Jordan, Syria & Lebanon

a Lonely Planet travel atlas

Jordan, Syria & Lebanon – travel atlas

1st edition

Published by
Lonely Planet Publications
Head Office: PO Box 617, Hawthorn, Vic 3122, Australia
Branches: 155 Filbert St, Suite 251, Oakland, CA 94607, USA
10 Barley Mow Passage, Chiswick, London W4 4PH, UK
71 bis rue du Cardinal Lemoine, 75005 Paris, France

Cartography
Steinhart Katzir Publishers Ltd
Fax: 972-3-699-7562
email: 100264.721@compuserve.com

Printed by
Colorcraft Ltd, Hong Kong

Photographs
Ann Jousiffe, Peter Jousiffe

Front Cover: Jerash, Jordan (Ann Jousiffe)
Back Cover: Souvenir seller, Petra, Jordan (Ann Jousiffe)
Title Page: Roman ruins at Baalbek, Lebanon (Ann Jousiffe)
Contents Page: Bread seller, Beirut, Lebanon (Ann Jousiffe)

First Published
January 1997

Although the authors and publisher have tried to make the information as accurate as possible, they accept no responsibility for any loss, injury or inconvenience sustained by any person using this book.

National Library of Australia Cataloguing in Publication Data
Jousiffe, Ann
Jordan, Syria & Lebanon travel atlas.

1st ed.
Includes index.
ISBN 0 86442 441 8

1. Jordan - Maps, Tourist. 2. Jordan - Road maps.
3. Syria - Road maps. 4. Syria - Maps, Tourist.
5. Lebanon - Maps, Tourist. 6. Lebanon - Road maps.
I. Jousiffe, Peter. II. Title. (Series : Lonely Planet travel atlas).

912.569

text & maps © Lonely Planet & Steinhart Katzir Publishers 1997
photos © photographers as indicated 1997

Contents

Ann Jousiffe

After spending a decade working in advertising, Ann escaped the rat race to work as a freelance writer and photographer specialising in the Middle East and North Africa. Based in London, she has written the Libya section of *North Africa – travel survival kit* and is now working on *Lebanon – travel survival kit*. Between spending her time in deserts and ancient ruins and working on documentaries, she leads tours to Libya and collapses in front of the television in her London flat with a glass or two of red wine.

Peter Jousiffe

Peter has travelled extensively around the Middle East and North Africa, indulging his passion for Islamic architecture and desert ruins. He now works as a freelance photojournalist and has recently worked in Libya, Bosnia and Lebanon, where he has been researching material for Lonely Planet's *Middle East on a Shoestring*.

About this Atlas

This book is another addition to the Lonely Planet travel atlas series. Designed to tie in with the equivalent Lonely Planet guidebooks, we hope that the *Jordan, Syria & Lebanon travel atlas* helps travellers enjoy their trip even more. As well as detailed, accurate maps, this atlas also contains a multilingual map legend, useful travel information in five languages, and a comprehensive index to ensure easy location-finding.

The maps were checked on the road by Ann and Peter Jousiffe as part of research conducted for a new edition of Lonely Planet's *Middle East on a shoestring* and for the upcoming *Lebanon – travel survival kit*.

From the Publishers

Thanks to Danny Schapiro, chief cartographer at Steinhart Katzir Publishers, who supervised production of this atlas. Danna Sharoni, Iris Sardes and Michal Pait-Benny were responsible for the cartography. Iris Sardes also prepared the index. At Lonely Planet, editorial checking of the maps and index was completed by Paul Smitz. Paul Clifton was responsible for the cartographic checking. Layout, design and cover design was completed by Louise Keppie-Klep. Paul Smitz edited the getting around section.

Lou Byrnes coordinated the translations. Thanks to translators Yoshi Abe, Chantal Boudrie, Christa Bouga-Hochstöger, Olivier Cirendini, Adrienne Costanzo, Pedro Diaz, Gunhild Henley, Sergio Mariscal, Isabelle Muller, Penelope Richardson and Karin Riederer.

Thanks also to Damien Simonis for helping out with the getting around section.

Request

This atlas is designed to be clear, comprehensive and reliable. We hope you'll find it a worthy addition to your Lonely Planet travel library. Even if you don't, please let us know! We'd appreciate any suggestions you may have to make this product even better. Please complete and send us the feedback page at the back of this atlas to let us know exactly what you think.

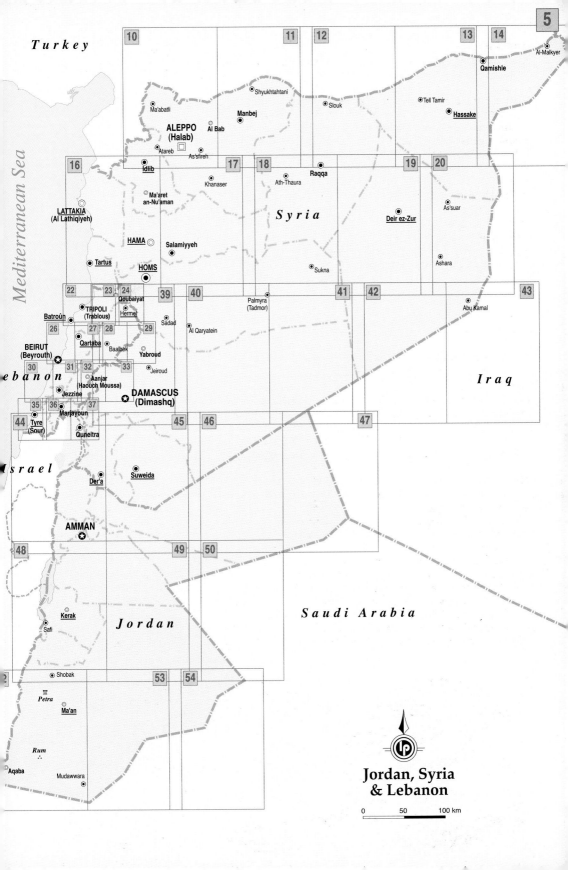

Turkey

Mediterranean Sea

5

| 10 | | | 11 | 12 | | | 13 | 14 |

Al-Malkyer

Qamishle

Shyukhtahtani

Ma'abatli

Manbej

Slouk

Tell Tamir

Hassake

**ALEPPO
(Halab)**

Al Bab

Atareb

As'sfireh

| 16 | | | 17 | 18 | | 19 | 20 |

Idlib

Raqqa

Khanaser

Ath-Thaura

As'suar

**Ma'aret
an-Nu'aman**

Syria

**LATTAKIA
(Al Lathiqiyeh)**

Deir ez-Zur

HAMA

Salamiyyeh

Ashara

Tartus

HOMS

Sukna

| 22 | | 23 | 24 | 39 | 40 | | 41 | 42 | | 43 |

Qoubaiyat

Palmyra
(Tadmor)

Abu Kamal

**TRIPOLI
(Trablous)**

Hermel

Batroûn

Sadad

| 26 | 27 | 28 | 29 |

Al Qaryatein

Qartaba

Baalbek

Iraq

Yabroud

| 30 | 31 | 32 | 33 |

Jeiroud

**BEIRUT
(Beyrouth)**

Aanjar
(Haouch Moussa)

Jezzine

**DAMASCUS
(Dimashq)**

Lebanon

| 35 | 36 | 37 |

Marjayoun

| 44 | **Tyre
(Sour)** | 45 | 46 | | 47 |

Quneitra

Israel

Der'a

Suweida

AMMAN

| 48 | | 49 | 50 |

Saudi Arabia

Kerak

Jordan

Safi

Shobak

| 53 | 54 |

Petra

Ma'an

Rum

Aqaba

Mudawwara

**Jordan, Syria
& Lebanon**

0   50   100 km

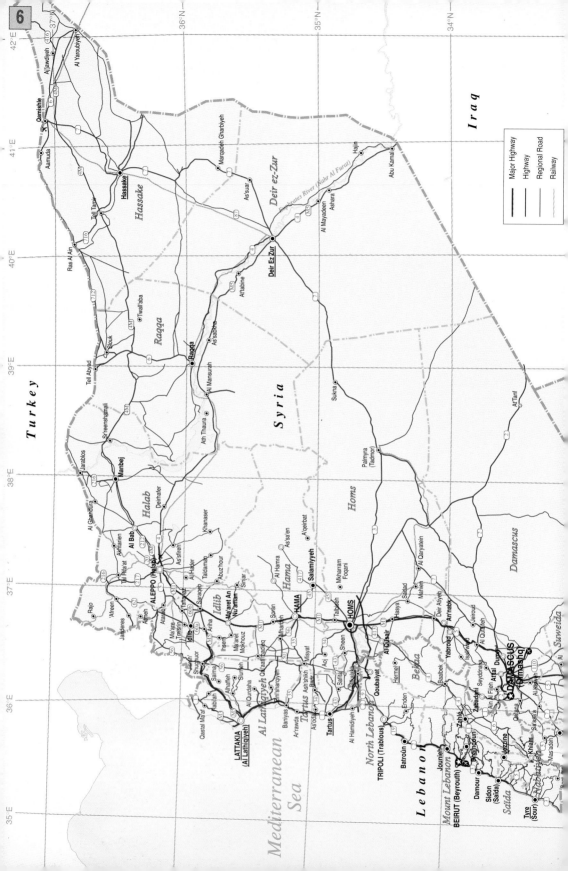

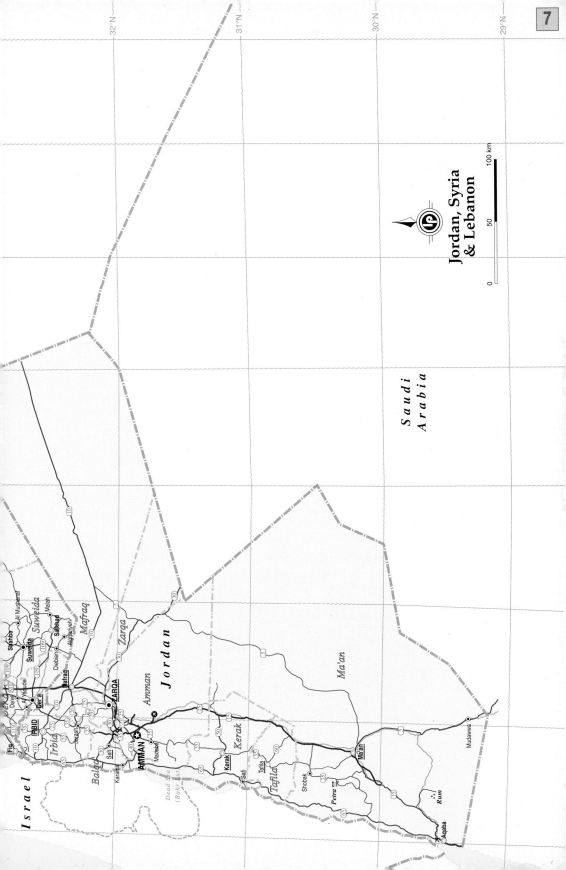

MAP LEGEND

Number of Inhabitants:

DAMASCUS	☐	>500,000
BEIRUT	◉	250,000 - 500,000
LATTAKIA	◎	100,000 - 250,000
Hermel	◉	50,000 - 100,000
Qoubaiyat	◎	25,000 - 50,000
Karama	◉	10,000 -25,000
Ibrez	○	<10000
Anbarli	◎	Village

AMMAN
Capital City
Capitale
Hauptstadt
Capital
首都

✪
Capital City (Locator map)
Capitale (Carte de situation)
Hauptstadt (Orientierungskarte)
Capital (Mapa Localizador)
首都 （地図上の位置）

IRBID
Provincial Capital
Capitale de Province
Landeshauptstadt
Capital de Provincia
地方の中心地

Machgara
District Headquarters
Quartier Général du District
Bezirkshauptquartier
Sede Central del Distrito
地区の本部

International Boundary
Limites Internationales
Staatsgrenze
Frontera Internacional
国境

Disputed Boundary
Frontière Contestée
umstrittene Grenze
Frontera Disputada
国境紛争境界線

Provincial Boundary
Limites de la Province
Landesgrenze
Frontera de Provincia
地方の境界

Ferry Route
Route de ferry
Fährroute
Transbordador
フェリーの航路

Major Highway
Route Nationale
Femstraße
Carretera Principal
主要な国道

Highway
Route Principale
Landstraße
Carretera
国道

Regional Road
Route Régionale
Regionale Fernstraße
Carretera Regional
地方道

Secondary Road
Route Secondaire
Nebenstraße
Carretera Secundaria
二級道路

Unsealed Road
Route non bitumée/piste
Unbefestigte Straße
Carretera sin Asfaltar
未舗装の道

Railway
Voie de chemin de fer
Eisenbahn
Ferrocarril
鉄道

Jerouf Station
Railway Station
Gare Ferroviaire
Bahnhof
Estación de Ferrocarril
駅

⊂55⊃
Route Number
Numérotation Routière
Routenummer
Ruta Número
道路の番号

99
Distance in Kilometres
Distance en Kilomètres
Entfernung in Kilometern
Distancia en Kilómetros
距離 （km）

✈ International Airport
    Aéroport International
    Internationaler Flughafen
    Aeropuerto Internacional
    国際空港

✈ Domestic Airport
    Aéroport National
    Inlandflughafen
    Aeropuerto Interior
    国内線空港

⛴ Seaport
    Port de Mer
    Seehafen
    Puerto Marítimo
    港

🗼 Lighthouse
    Phare
    Leuchtturm
    Faro
    灯台

☪ Mosque
    Mosquée
    Moschee
    Mezquita
    モスク

† Church
    Église
    Kirche
    Iglesia
    教会

Castle/Fort
    Château/Château Fort
    Burg/Festung
    Castillo/Fuerte
    城・砦

∴ Ruins
    Ruines
    Ruinen
    Ruinas
    遺跡

Phoenician Ruins
    Ruines phóniciennes
    phönizische Ruinen
    Ruinas Fenicias
    フェニキアの廃墟

🏛 Classical Ruins
    Ruines antiques
    klassische Ruinen
    Ruinas Clásicas
    古典ギリシャの廃墟

Arab Ruins
    Ruines Arabes
    arabische Ruinen
    Ruinas Árabes
    アラブの廃墟

Crusader Ruins
    Site Croisé
    Kreuzritterruinen
    Ruinas de las Cruzadas
    十字軍の廃墟

✳ Viewpoint
    Point de Vue
    Aussicht
    Mirador
    展望地点

Harf Sannine
2628 + Mountain
    Montagne
    Berg
    Montaña
    山

⌂ Cave
    Grotte
    Höhle
    Cueva
    洞窟

National Park
    Parc National
    Nationalpark
    Parque Nacional
    国立公園

Beach
    Plage
    Strand
    Playa
    海岸

River
    Fleuve/Rivière
    Fluß
    Río

Wadi
    Wadi
    Wadi
    Uadi
    ワジ

Lake
    Lac
    See
    Lago
    湖

Spring/Well
    Source/Puits
    Quelle/Brunnen
    Manantial/Pozo
    泉

Waterfall
    Cascades
    Wasserfall
    Cascada
    滝

Swamp
    Marais
    Sumpf
    Pantano
    沼地

Desert
    Désert
    Wüste
    Desierto
    砂漠

2500 m
2100 m
1800 m
1500 m
1200 m
900 m
600 m
300 m
150m
0
-150m
-300m

0   15   30 km

Jordan & Syria 1 : 700 000

0   5   10 km

Lebanon 1 : 200 000

Projection: Universal Transverse Mercator

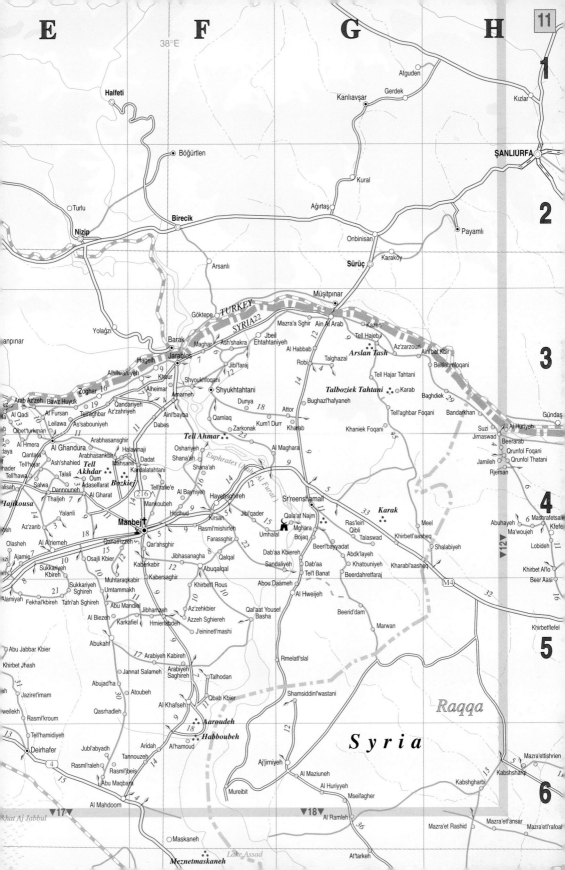

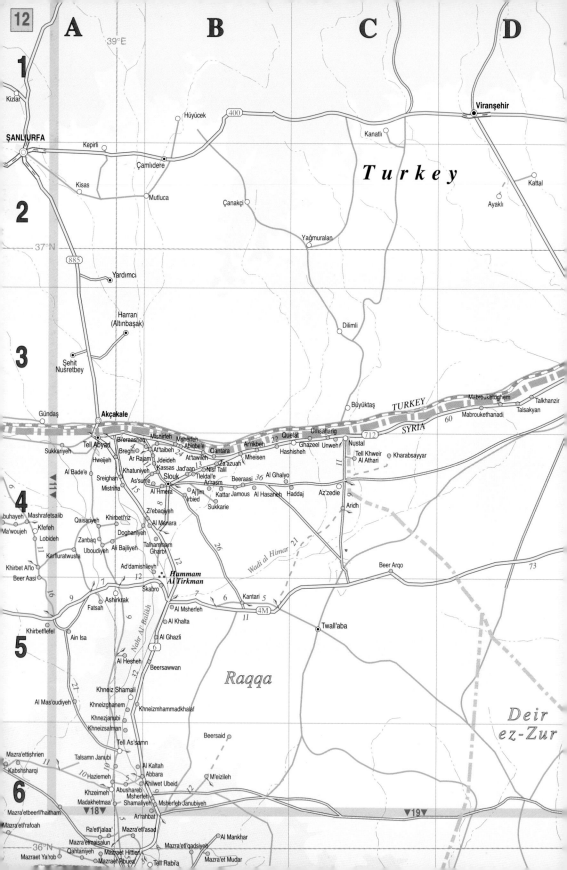

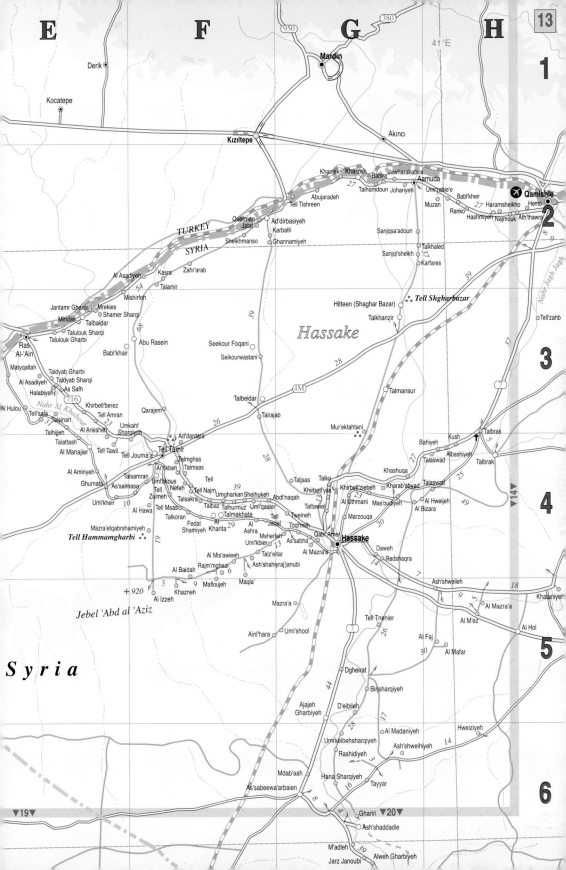

PETER AND ANN JOUSIFFE

PETER JOUSIFFE

ANN JOUSIFFE

Top: Sunset over Palmyra (Tadmor), Syria
Middle: 1943 vintage Ksara made in Zahlé, Lebanon
Bottom: Beiteddine Palace, Lebanon

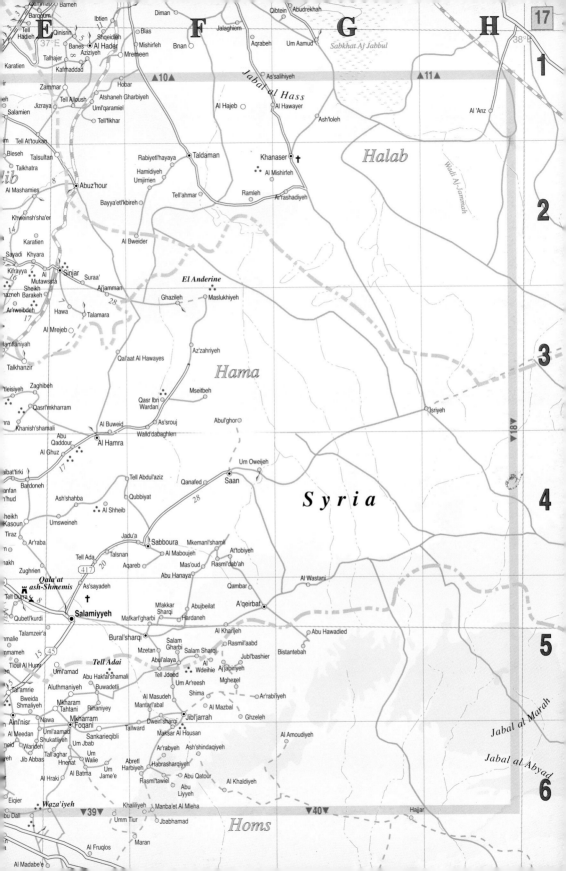

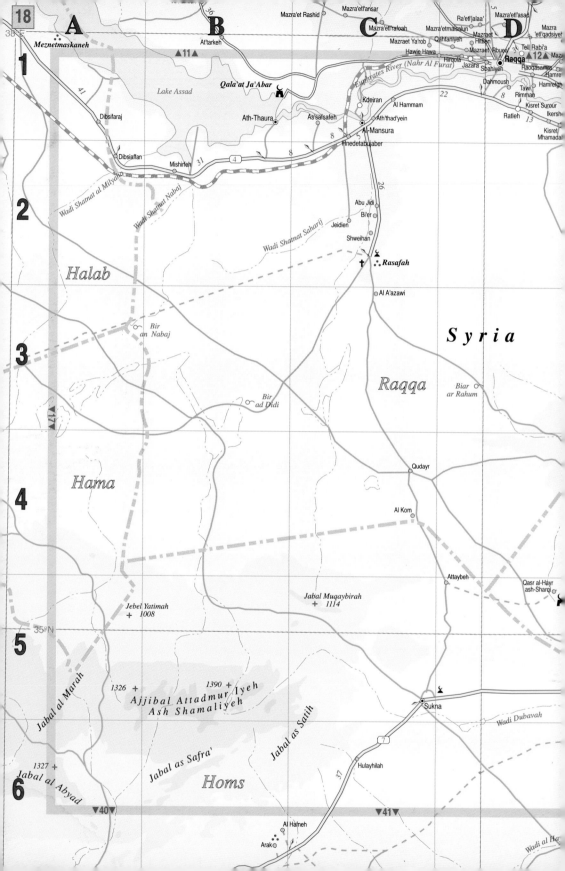

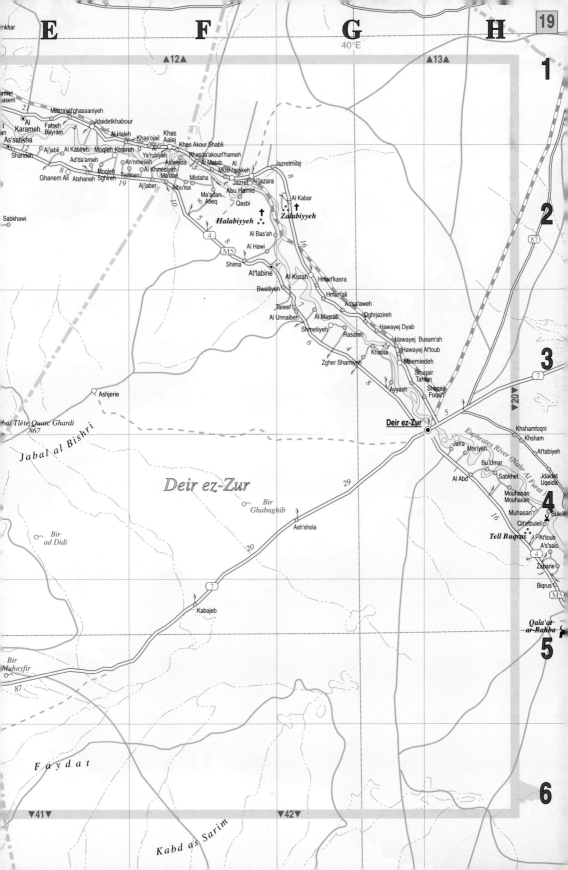

40°E

1

2

3

4

5

6

▲12▲   ▲13▲

nkhar
asem
E
21
Al
Karameh
As'sabkha
12
Shandeh
Mazra'ell'ghassaniyeh
Fatseh
Bayram
Jdaidetkhabour
Al Haleh
Khas'ojail
Khas
Aalej
Khas Akour Shabli
Aj'jabli   Al Kabireh
Moqleh Kbiereh
Al
Ya'rubiyeh
Khasda'akourl'hameh
Ad'da'ameh
An'nmeseh
As'weida   Al Malab   Al
Mushtarakeh
Jazretmilaj
Ghanem Ali   Atshaneh Sghireh
Tishrien
Al Khmesiyeh
Ma'dan
Mistaha
Jazret Aj'jazara
Moqleh   19
Aj'jaber
Albu'isa
Ma'adan
Afieq
Abu Hamid
Qasbi
Al Kabar
10
5
† Halabiyyeh
† Zalabiyyeh
Sabkhawi
Al Bas'ah
4
8
Al Hawi
M5
16
Shima
At'tabine
Al Kisrah   Hmarl'kasra
Bweitiyeh
Hmarl'ali
Tareef   7
As'sa'aweh
Al Unnaibeh   Al Masrab
Dghrjazireh
Shmetiyeh
Hawayej Dyab
Rasafeh
Hawayej Busam'ah
Zgher Shamiyeh   4
Kharita
Hawayej At'toub
8
Mhemiedeh
Shuqair
Tahtan
Ayyash
Shuqair
Foqah
Ashjerie
bal Tléte Quatc Ghardi
867
Jabal al Bishri
Deir ez-Zur
5
Deir ez-Zur
Khshamfoqni
Khsham
Jafra
Euphrates River (Nahr Al Furat)
Bir
Ghabaghib
Mre'iyeh
At'tabiyeh
29
Bir
ad Didi
Bu Umar
Al Abd
Sabkhet
Jdaidel
Uqeida
Ash'shola
Mouhasan
Mouhasan
Muhasan
4
Bulei
Qit'etbuleil
20
Tell Buqras
At'toub   A's'salo
7
Zabarie
Kabajeb
Biqrus
M5
Qala'at
ar-Rahba
Bir
Muhayfir
87

F a y d a t

▼41▼   ▼42▼

K a b d   a s   S a r i m

87

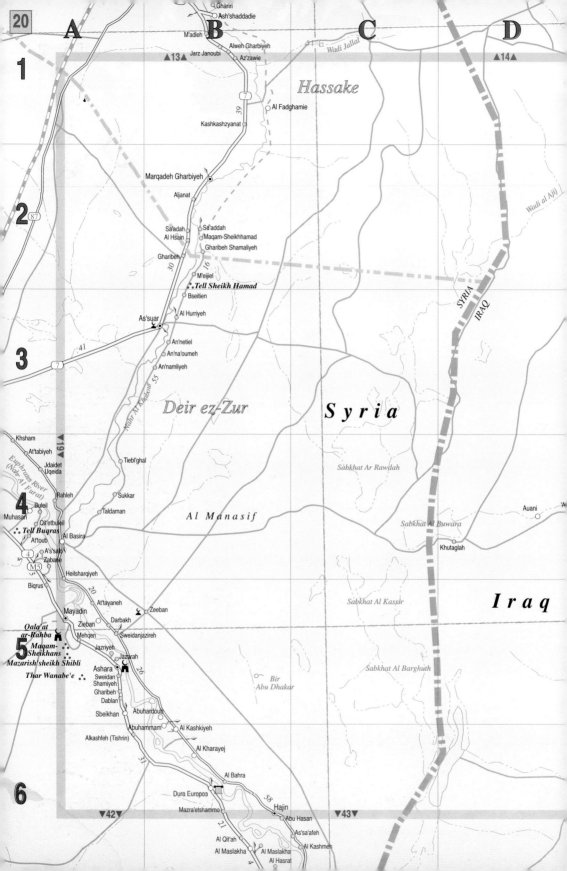

A   **B**   **C**   **D**

1

2

3

4

5

6

Gharin
Ash'shaddadie
M'adleh
Alweh Gharbiyeh
Jarz Janoubi
Az'zawie
Wadi Jallal
▲13▲
▲14▲

Hassake

Al Fadghamie
Kashkashzyanat

Marqadeh Gharbiyeh
Aljanat

Sa'adah
Sa'addah
Al Hsain
Maqam-Sheikhhamad
Gharibeh Shamaliyeh
Gharibeh
M'eijiel
Tell Sheikh Hamad
Bseitien
As'suar
Al Hurriyeh
An'netiel
An'na'oumeh
An'namliyeh

Deir ez-Zur

S y r i a

Nahr Al Khabour

SYRIA
IRAQ

Wadi al Ajij

Khsham
At'tabiyeh
▼19▼
Jdaidet
Uqeida
Tiebl'ghal
Rahleh
Buleil
Sukkar
Muhasan
Qit'etbuleil
Taldaman
Tell Buqras
Al Basira
At'toub
A's'sakl
Zabane
Heilsharqiyeh
Biqrus
At'tayaneh
Zeeban
Mayadin
Darbakh
Zieban
Qala'at ar-Rahba
Mehqen
Sweidanjazireh
Maqam-Sheikhans
Jazriyeh
Mazarish'sheikh Shibli
Jazarah
Ashara
Thar Wanabe'e
Sweidan Shamiyeh
Gharibeh
Dablan
Sbeikhan
Abuhardoub
Abuhammam
Al Kashkiyeh
Alkashfeh (Tishrin)
Al Kharayej

Al Manasif

Sabkhat Ar Rawdah

Sabkhat Al Buwara
Auani
Khutaglah

Sabkhat Al Kassir

I r a q

Sabkhat Al Barghuth

Bir Abu Dhakar

Al Bahra
Dura Europos
Mazra'etshammo
Hajin
Abu Hasan
▼42▼
▼43▼
Al Qit'ah
As'sa'afeh
Al Maslakha
Al Kashmen
Al Maslakha
Al Hasrat

Beirut's landmark Pigeon Rocks, Lebanon

A   **B**   **C**   **D**

1

▲16▲

2

Mediterranean Sea

3

Palmier Island
Ramkine Island   *Sanâni Island*
Toûroûs Island
Taouîlé Island   *Laoukas Island*
Mdoura Island
Bella Island
Baqar Island

El Minie

Deir Aamar   Hrai

Al Mina   El Beddaoui   30

Jabal Tourbal
605   Kaf
+ 162

Bousit
Ain el Faouar   Hilar

TRIPOLI
(Trablous)   *Ain*
Aalma   Miryata
28   El Qadriye

Majdelya   Zgharta   Arde   Aachach
162   Rachaain
El Bahsas   Aasscun   Rachain
Karabach   Kfar Hata   Kfar Dlaqous

4

El Qalamoun   Ras Masqa
ech Chmaliya
Ras Masqa   Kfar Maoura
ej Jnoubiye
Kfar Zeina   27

Dedde   Barsa   Kfar Chakhna   *Ard el Mo*
Batroumine
Qalhat   *Ez Zeharta*   26   Bsibaal   Beit Daoud   *El Baaz*

5

Enfe   Fiaa
Bdibba   Kfar Yachit
Btourram   Kfar Sghab   867   *el*
Chekka   Aafsidiq   Bsarma   Aarjess
305   Daraiya   Bnichaai   Mizi
Ras Ach Chekka   *Ouadi el Koura*   Hmais
Bechmezzine   Kfar Fou

50   Kfar Hazir   *Dahr ech Choumar*   Raskifa   Sebaal   Mazra
El Heri   Kfar Aaqqa   Karm Sadde   Aitou   et Toul
Amioun   Kousba   *Jabal Aito*

6

Nahr el Assfour
Hamat   Kifraiya   Ain Akrine   Moghr el Ahoual   Serraal   Aarbet Qozt
Ras   350   Rechdibbine   765
▼26▼   Nhach   Kfar Hata   + 336   401   Tourza
Batroûn   Koubba   ▼27▼   Bziza   804   Barhalioun   Aabdine
186   424   Btaaboura   Metrit   1374   Beit Menzer   Bla
Jabal Aabrine   Kaftoun   Dar Baachtar
Rachkida   331   Boqsmaiya   El Majdel   Qnat
Aabrine   Deir Billa   + 853

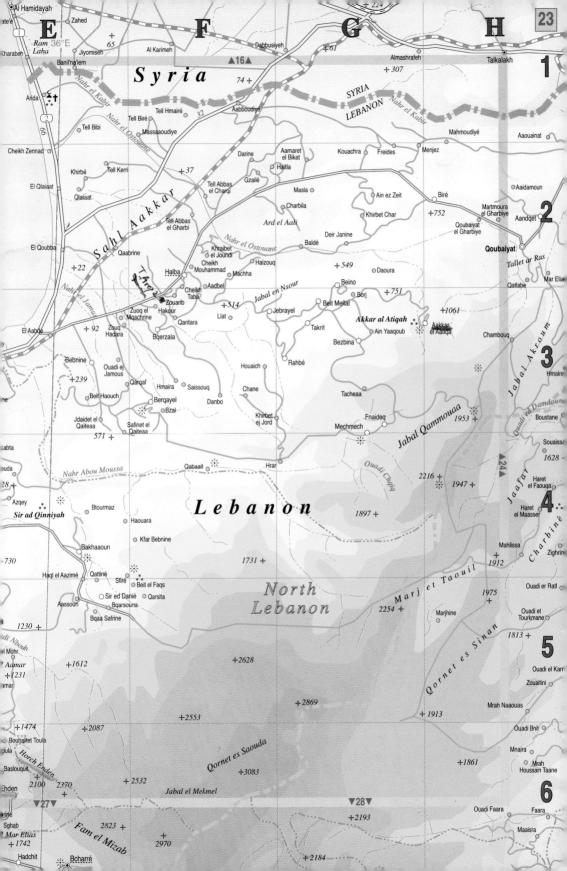

A   **B**   **C**   **D**

1

Um Hartien   502 +   Dnebel   Az'zafaraneh

Nasriye   Zahabiyeh   Khiebetl'hamam   Mshahdeh

Braghit   Oum Jame   ▲16▲   Ratyet L'bahra

Msheirfeh   Hdaideh   Khirbet Ghazi   Qattinah

Machta Hammoud   401 +   Qubti   Wajhil'bahr

Nahr el Kabir

Aaouainat   Chadra   Hmairat   *Lake Homs*

Machta Hassan   822 +   Ouadi Khaled   Qarha   Jobatiyeh   Kafer Abdah

Aaidamoun   Hnaider   Obien   Daminah Algharbia

2

Aandqet   Qenia   +734   An'naem   *Homs*

North Lebanon   Al Sahr   Soummaqiyate

Jabal Akroum

Qoubaiyat   +830   Tell Nabi Mend (Kadesh)   Kafr Mousa

Tallet ar Ras   Kfartoun   Al Hoz   Arjoun

Qatlabe   Mar Elias   Akroum   Hweik   Dabaa   583 +

Jabal el Houssain   Ouadi Hanna   Aarabiye

3

Jabal Akroum   Hmaire   +985   **S y r i a**   +510   Qusayr   413

Ouadi el Damdoun   Boustane   Hariqa   Sahlat el Ma   +653   Kokran

Fissane   Qasr   Al Ma'neyh   As'safsafeh   Al Qusair

Souaissa   Charbiné   Kouakh   +584   Hammam   Ad'dayabiyeh

1628 +   ▼23▼   Charbine el Faouqa   *SYRIA*

4

Jaafar   Haret el Faouqa   Nassiriya   *LEBANON*   Ramleh

Haret el Maasser   Zighrine et Tahta   Bouaida   534 +   Al Ubudiyeh

Mahlissa   Zighrine   **L e b a n o n**   Mazraat Beit et Tachm   Jusieh

Ouadi er Ratl   *Ard el Kroum*   *Nahr el Assi*   *Ard el Qamar*   Jouar   4   Josiyetl'khrab

5

Ouadi et Tourkmane   *Bekaa*   **Hermel**   Chouaghir   +649   *Jabal Hass*

+813   Mrah Beit Alaoui   Ras el Assi

Ouadi el Karm   Zouaitini   *Ouadi el Karm*   Mazraat Ain ez Zarqa   656 +   *Marbaa el Banjakiÿe*

Mrah Naaouas   Qaa

6

Ouadi Bnit   *Ard el Kneisse*   Mrah en Nahr   +767   +1457   *Jabal Jumr*

Inaira   Mrah Houssain Taane

Faara   Mrah Bekdach   Mhattet Ras Baalbek   ▼28▼   ▼29▼   *Ras Baalbek ech Charqi*

Maaisra   +880   *Ard er Ras*   Ras Baalbek   1642 +   *Jabal Haouerta*   1401 +

Nahr el Assi   12   *Ouadi Haouerta*   Khirbet al-Agha

The spectacular ruined Nabataean capital of Petra, Jordan

| A | B | C | D |

1
2
3
4
5
6

Mediterranean Sea

186 +424 *Jabal Aabrine*
Rachkida
Aabrine
▲22▲
Bijdarfel
427 +
Eddé
Jrane
Ghouma
Nahr Madfoun
+519
Aabdellé
Toula
430 + Maad
Bejjé
Gharzouz
Heloué
Ghalbou
Monsef
Hsarat
Amchit
Ouadi Eddé
Bentaael

Byblos
(Jbail)
Nahr el Joura
993 +
Blat
Ouadi el Dargé
Jabal Haou
11
Nhar el Fidar
Jouret
el Qattine
Halat
Nahr Ibrahim
Ado
Nahr Ibrahim
Zaaitra
Yahchou
Aabeidat
Ouadi el Ghabour
Buoar
Ghbale
Safra
+970
Tabarja
Kfour
Chah
+526
Hayata
Larnaca
Jdaidet
Ghazir
Aaramoun 1485
Casino du Liban
Ghazir
Rachiîne
Maameltain
+863
Dlebta
Bay of Jounieh
Ghnanaair
34°E
Ghosta
Haret Sakhr
Aachqout
Ras et Tair
Jounieh
Harissa
Raifoun
Fai
Ghadir
Daraaoun
1218
Kaslit
Zouq Mkaye
Sarba
Qlaiaat
Zouq Mosbeh
Aintoura
Aajaltoun
Ouadi Daraiy
Nahr el Kelb
Jeitta
Zabbou
Nahr el Kelb
Hamlaya
Dbaiyé
Jeitta Grotto
Kf
Aad
Beit ech Chaar
Beit Chebab
Bteghrir
Antelias
Bikfaya
BEIRUT
(Beyrouth)
St. Georges
Bolonia
Bay
Dall ed Dib
Qornet
Chehoune
Choueir
21
Ras Beyrouth
Zalga
Bsalim
Nabay
Bharsaf
Douar
Beirut
Bourj
Hammoud
Nahr Antelias
Jouret el
Ballout
Dahr as
Souane
Qaaqour
Mt
Jdaidé
Ain Saadé
Broummana
Baabdat
880 +
Dékouané
Aarbanîyé
Salima
▼30▼
Mansouriyé
Beit Meri
▼31▼
Jnah
Mkalless
Qssaibe
Arsoun
Jouar
el
Hazmiyé
+732
Ras el
Meth
Deir el Harf
Qornayel
Ouzaa
Mraije
Yarzé
Nahr Beyrouth

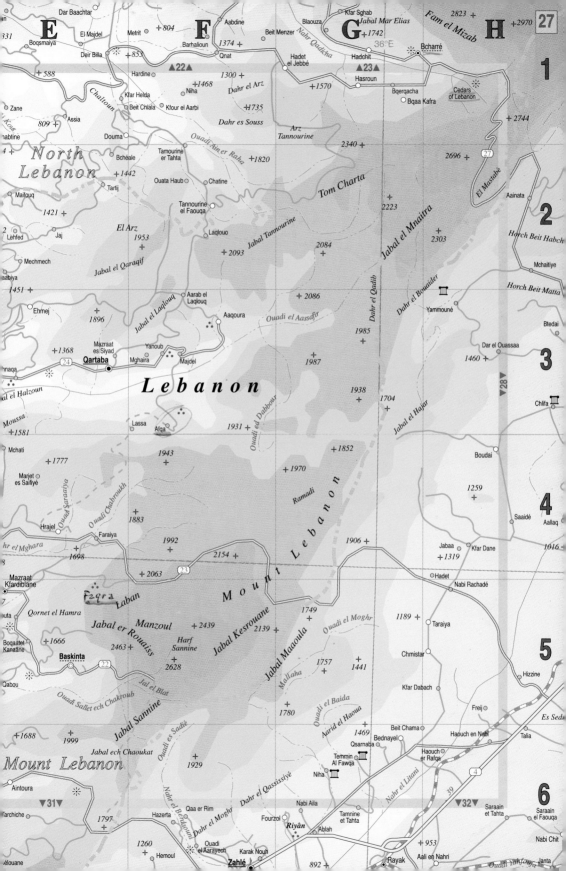

A   B   C   D

1

2193

+2184

▲23▲

▲24▲

Ouadi Faara

Faara

Maaisra

Halbata

Ras Baalbek

Jdaide

Fakehe

112

El Mastabé

Kharayeb   Zabboud

Mrah
el Aabed

Mrah
el Chaab

Jabboulé

+894

El Ain

1911

1580

Sbouba

Harbata

Bejjajé

Nabi Osmane

+1646

Jabal el En

2

Aainata

Nabha el Qeddam

1150

Mrah Harfouch

Nabha

+991

Toufiqiyé

Laboué

Aan

Horch Beit Habchi

Qarha

1306 +

Riha

Moqraq

Mchaitiye

Zrazir

Bechouat

Safra

Chmis el Maaisra

Horch Beit Matta

Btedai

Deir el Ahmar

Knaissé

Chaat

29

Ras el Hadet

L e b a n o n

1821

+

3

Chlifa

27

4

1118

Maqné

Younine

1744 +

Jabal Younine

1863 +

Ouadi el Boura

Jouar en Naqr

Ouadi en Nahlé

4

27

Iaat

Nahlé

Ard el Kichek

Aallaq

Haouch
Tell Safiyé

1016 +

Haouch Barada

Baalbek

✝

+2393

LEBANON

SYRIA

+2383

31°N

Majdaloun

Ain
Bourday

Jourd Nahlé

Douris

2128

S y r i a

5

Hizzine

2183

2424

2417

Bekaa

Es Sedr

Taibé

1591

Talia

Britel

1256

Nabi Sbat

1961

Haour Taala

Ram el Kibch

6

Khodr

1144

▼32▼

Ram el Marjouha

▼33▼

Aassal el Ouard

Saraain
el Faouqa

+1447

Ham

2111

Isall'ward

Nabi Chit

Khraibé

Jabal Chmiss

A n t i   L e b a n o n

(Jabal Lubnan Al-Sharqi)

Janta

Maarboun

Tfail

E
F
G
H

1476 +
+ 464

Jabal Haouerta
Ras Baalbek ech Charqi
+ 1642
Ouadi Haouerta
1401 +
Khirbet al-Agha
▲ 24 ▲
▲ 39 ▲

1

+ 1578
1612 +
Jabal Maouassel

+ 1589
Dhour el Khanzir
+ 1903

589

Halimet Qarah
+ 2173
1601 +

2

Ouadi Murtabiya

+ 1852
Qala'at el Hosn
LEBANON
1504 +

1942 +
SYRIA
Dahr el Haoua

3

8

+ 2285
Ouadi al-Khashiyaa
Ouadi al-Khurba
Ouadi Makhra
Deir Atiyeh

+ 2629
Jarajir
+ 1642

+ 2616
Jabal el Atnein
Al Mishrfeh
(Fletah)

S y r i a

4

1895 +
As'sahl
An'nabk
39

Damascus

5

Ras Al Ma'arra
Yabroud

Ras Al Ain

Aj'jibeh

Khansinan Pasha

6

▼ 33 ▼
▼ 39 ▼
As'sarkha
S
M1

A   B   C   D

1

2

3

Mediterranean Sea

4

5

6

▲ 26 ▲

Ras el Mousri

Damour

N. ed Da

Ras es Saadiyat   Saadiyat

12   Dahr
el Mghara

Nhar N.

• Jiyé

Baassir

*Ras en
Nabi Younés*   Barja   Marj

Ouadi ez Zeini

Ras en
Nabi Younés   Dalhoun

10   402 +

Sibline   33

Ouardaniye   Keterma

Ras Saharé   • Rmaité   Mghairiyé

Ouadi Holaya   Majdalouna

• Haret Aalman   Joun

Nahr el Awwali

Bramiyé   Moun

Danayé

Sidon   Hababiyé
Saida
Hara   • Aabra   • Karkha
Ras Abarouh   Majdelyoun   Salhiyé

34

35   Lebaa   Kfar
+ 316
Ain ed Delb   517
Miyé   Qraiyé   Baissour
ou Miyé

• Dart es Sim   **Al Janu**

Tanbourit

Maghdouche   Maidel

Ghaziye   36   Kfar Hatta

Qinnarit   452 +   Kfar

Nahr Saitanik   *Ouad*

232 +   Aanqoum

Aaqtanit   Bnaafoul   406   Jernaya
+

Maamariyé   Houmine
Aaddoussiyé   Najjariya   5   Haljé   et Tahta

▼ 35 ▼   Maknouniyé   ▼ 36 ▼   572 +   Sa

3   Arkey   Roumine
Ras ech Chaq   Aazzé
Merouaniyé   Bfaroua   Hmailé

Sarafand   228   Zefta   Dei
(Sareptal)   +   Toufahta   **Nabatiyeh**   ez Zah
+ 153
Baissariyé

A   **B**   **C**   **D**

1

+ 1260

Hazerta
Dahr el Moghr
Riyân
Ablah
Saraaïn et Tahta
Saraaïn el Faouqa

+ Hemoul
Ouadi el Aarayech
Karak Nouh
39
Aali en Nahri
Janta
Yahfc

Zahlé
36°E
892
Rayak
▲27▲
Ouadi Yahfoufa
▲28▲

Maallaga

Dahr ech Chir

+ 1441

Jdita
Deir el Ghazal
Raite
1346 +
+ 1669

Bouarej
Chitaura
Saadnayel
Kousaya
+ 1621

13
2
Taalabaya
Terbol
Alieb

Qabb Elias
Sahm et Tourkmane
4
Ksar el Aabd
1464 +

18
Jabal Terbol
Ain Kfar Zabad
1777

2

Chebreqiyé
Barr Elias
+ 1220
Kfar Zabad
Er Rouss

+ 870
Er Marj
+ 1000
Ouadi Ain el Kharzir

19
Istubl
Jabal ech Charqi
1777

17
+ 913
+ 1180

Haouch el Harmé
8
+ 1395
LEBANON
Zabadani
Bloudan

Nahr el Ghzayel
Dekweh
Aanjar
(Haouch Moussa)
SYRIA
Ajjirjaniyeh

3

Majde Aanjar
1
Kfeiryabus
Buqqein

Chebreqiye
Souairi
+ 1475
5

+ 1393
Madaya

L e b a n o n
Hrerah

+ 1197
Ar'rawdah

10
Jdaidetyabous
Al Hosh

Aita el Foukhar
Batroûné
3

4

▼31▼
+ 1596
25
Soqwadibarada

Soultane Yaacoub et Faouqa
Chmiss Ouakr ed Dabaa
1489
+ 1530
4

Soultane Yaacoub et Tahta
+ 1243
Yanta
1375 +

Mooukha
Bakka
+ 1301
7

Biré
1222
1713
Maazar
Maysaloun

5

6
+ 1218
1624
+
+
Ain el Ajassa
Ras al Ain
Ad'dimas

12
Ain Aarab
Bekaa
+ 1634
Sahel Alsah

Kfar Danis
Khirbet Rouha
1679
Deir el Aachaer
Ya'four

Dahr el Ahmar
+
Jabal el Maazar
19

Kfar Qouq

6

+ 1288
Rakhleh

Aaqbé
+
2536

Rachaiya
Aaiha
+ 1664
Barqash
+ 1603
Sabboura

+ 1359
1625 +
Kafr Qouq
Jabal Antar
+ 1207

Ouadi el Maaber
2154 +
34
Aisaml'foqa
▼39▼

▼37▼
Qatana

E   F   G   H

1

2

3

4

5

6

Chmiss

Ham

Maarboun

+ 2111

Tfail

▲28▲

Ain
el Jaouza

Isall'ward

▲29▲

12

Hosharab

arghaya

Ouadi al-Farnas

Sahel en Njassa

Al Ma'mura

4

+ 1837

Al Jamiyeh

3

5

A'qobar

20

+ 1910

Syria

Rankous

6

Hafirl Foqa

8

+ 2095

Saydnaya

2

Talfita

Sahel Saydnaya

3

3

Ma'aret
Seidnaya

4

Bada

39

+ 1487

Damascus

5

Halbun

Mnien

Ainl'saheb

Ad'dreij

Ouadi Halboun

Deir

'Ain al-Fijeh

Ma'runeh

Hafirt'tahta

6

Nahr Barada

4

Ashrafiet
Alwadi

1087
+

1085 +

M1

Ad'drug

At'tal

Maaraba

6

Barzeh

Duma

Ash'shaffunieh

12

Al Hameh

19

Harasta

9

Jdaidetl'wadi

Al
Qaboun

Arbeen

Autaya

Quadsayya

Qummar

+ 1149

Jaoubar

Zamalka

Haz'zeh

Jobar

Jisrain

Kafrabatna

Ouadi al-Ahra

1085 +

□ **DAMASCUS**
(Dimashq)

Messe

Nahr Barada

An'nashabiyeh

13

Jeramâna

Al Mleiha

Zabdeen

Deir el A'safeer

▼39▼

7

Babbila

As'sayidah

Ma'adamiyeh

4

Kfar Sôûssé

Darayya

Zeinab

5

Jdaidetartouz

As'sbenijhzeinab

Part of the citadel which dominates the city of Aleppo, Syria

Mediterranean Sea

Ras ech Chaq
Merouahiye
35
Saraland (Sarepta)
153 +
228 +
Baissariyé

▲30▲
Satsakiyé
Tell el Mantara
Babliyé
1
Minet Abou Zebel
Qraiyé
Ghassaniyé
+332
Kaoutariyet es Siyad
Insariyé
Mazraat Iskandarouna
Khartoum
Aadloun
Oussamiyat
Sari
Nabatiyeh

Ras Minet Bou Zeid
Mazzrat Kaoutaniyet er Rézz
181 +
Insar
37
Ouadi el Ouata
+145
Aabba
2
+36
Matanayet ech Choumar
Kharayeb
Zrariyé
Ras Nabaa Mheilib
+248
10
12
Arzay
Nahr el Litani
Borj el Haoua
Qsaibé
Ras Minet Chourane
Tair Filsay
Sir el Gharbiyé
+388
Bourghliyé
Borj Rahhal
Deir Qanoun en Nahr
Halloussiyé
Ras Siddine el Bahr
146 +
Aabbassiyé
38
Chahour
Maaroub
Tair Semhat
Jannata
21
Derdghaiya
Srifa
Hammadiyé
Tair Debba
Maaraké
Barich
El Bass
303 +
3
Bafliyé
Tyre (Sour)
Salaa
Deir Kifa
L e b a n o n
Ras Minet er Rass
Debaal
Borj ech Chimali
Yannouh
15
Bazouriyé
39
▶36▼
Tair Zebna
Kfar Dounine
Rachidiyé
Ain Baal
16
Ras el Ain
Batouliyé
Hannaouiyé
Aaitanit
Jouaiya
Mjadel
Qana
Ouadi el Hariq
Saida
Mahroouna
Deir Ntar
Rmadiyé
+48
Qlailé
Chaaitiyé
Deir Aamess
4
Siddiqine
Ouadi ech Chmali
Ouadi el Ouazi
Karfra
Haris
Mansoura
Ouadi en Nahla
764 +
Haddata
Ras el Biyada
Zabqine
Jabal en Nassi
Yater
Ouadi ed Debb
Ras ed Dreijat
Majdel Zoun
Srobbine
Ouadi Ain ech Chamaa
Ouadi Ain Tiné
Rachaf
Chamaa
371 +
5
Tairé
Ras el Miassi
Chihine
757 +
Beit Lif
Debel et Emmeya
Ras el Baghlat
15
Tair Harfa
Qouzah
Naqoura
Aalma ech Chaab
Dhaira
Yarine
Ramiyé
Hanine
Labbouné
Marouahine
+713
Ras en Naqoura
+357
3
LEBANON
ISRAEL
Aaita ech Chaab
Akhziv
8
Nahal Bezet
Shelomi
Rmaich
+815
4
I s r a e l
6
70
35
Fassuta
89
Nahariya ●
5
Ma'alot Tarshiha
16
Nahal Kziv
Nahal Ga'aton

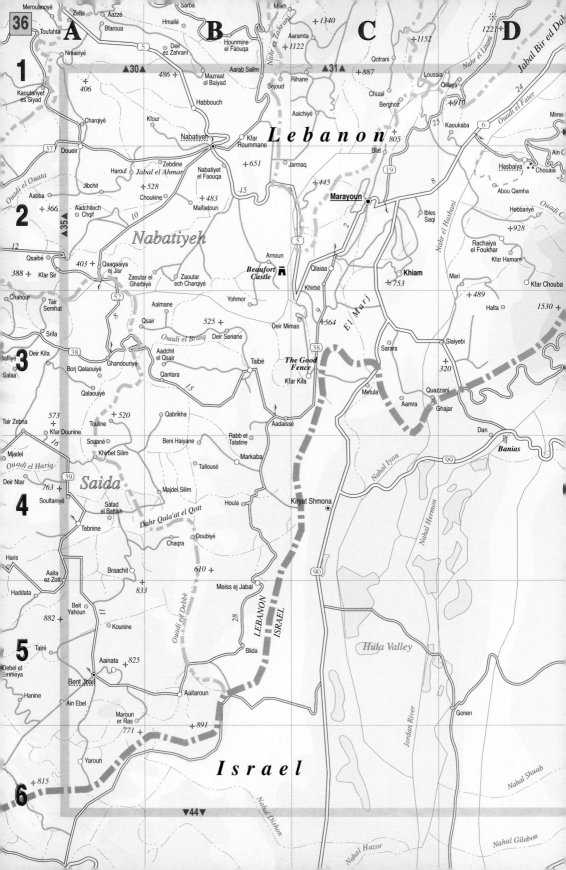

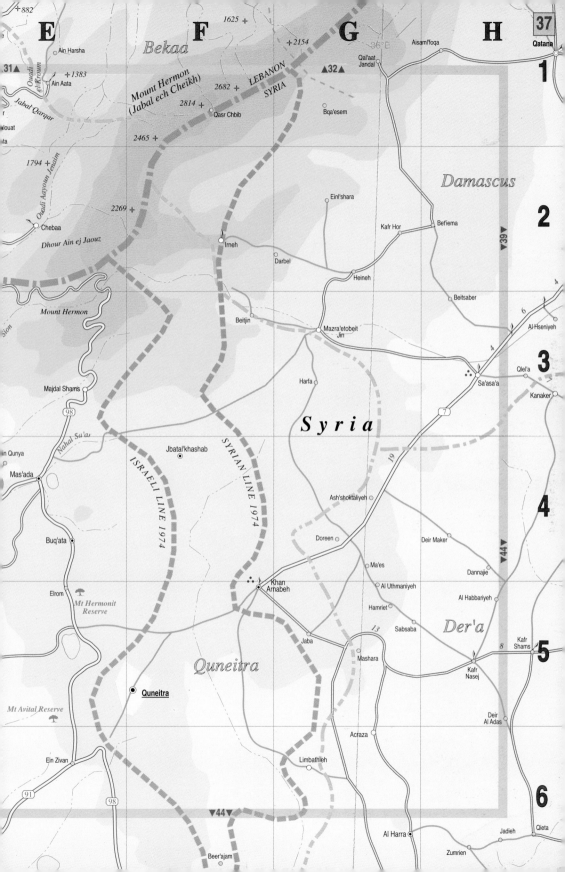

E   F   G   H

1
2
3
4
5
6

Bekaa

+882

◦ Ain Harsha

31▲

+1383
◦ Ain Aata

Jabal Qarqar

alouat
ta

+1794
Ouadi Aayoun Jenaim

◦ Chebaa

Dhour Ain ej Jaouz

Mount Hermon

in Qunya

◦ Mas'ada

98

Nahal Sa'ar

◦ Buq'ata

◦ Elrom

Mt Hermonit
Reserve

Mt Avital Reserve

◦ Ein Zivan

91   98

▼44▼

◦ Beer'ajam

1625 +

Mount Hermon
(Jabal ech Cheikh)

2682 +

2814 +

◦ Qasr Chbib

2465 +

2269 +

Irneh

Beitjin ◦

Majdal Shams

ISRAELI LINE 1974

◦ Jbatal'khashab

SYRIAN LINE 1974

◦ Khan
Arnabeh

Quneitra

◦ **Quneitra**

+2154

▲32▲

LEBANON
SYRIA

96°E

◦ Bqa'esem

◦ Einl'shara

Kafr Hor

Darbel ◦

Heineh ◦

Mazra'etobeit
Jin

Harfa ◦

Ash'shoktaliyeh ◦

Doreen ◦

Ma'es ◦

◦ Al Uthmaniyeh

Jaba ◦

13

Mashara ◦

Limbathieh ◦

Acraza ◦

◦ Al Harra

◦ Aisaml'foqa

Qal'aat
Jandal

Qatana

Damascus

Bet'iema

◦ Beitsaber

39▲

6

4

◦ Al Hseniyeh

4

Sa'asa'a

Qlel'a

7

Kanaker

19

◦ Deir Maker

44▲

◦ Dannajie

Hamriet ◦

Sabsaba ◦

◦ Al Habbariyeh

Der'a

Kafr
Nasej

8   Kafr
Shams

◦ Deir
Al Adas

Zumrien ◦

Jadieh ◦

Qieta ◦

Syria

PETER JOUSIFFE

Carpet seller in Aleppo, Syria

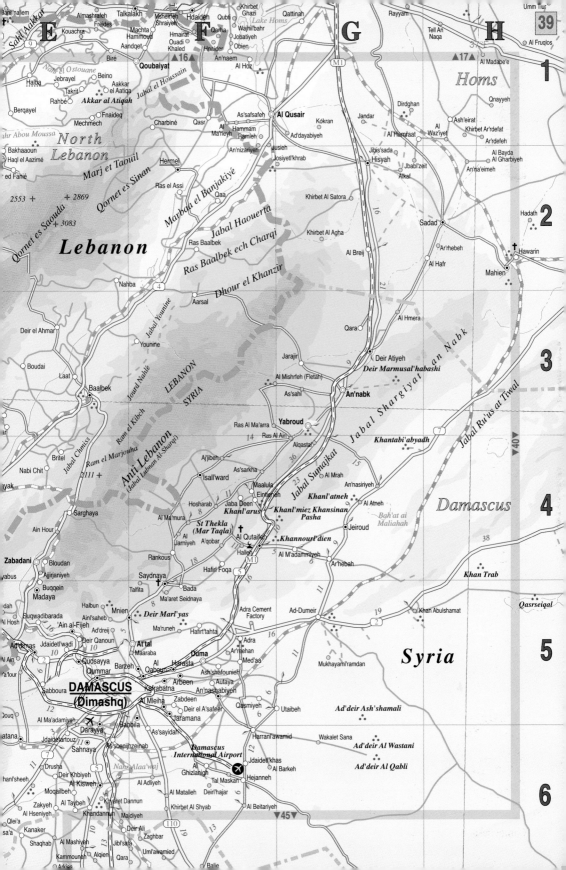

Umm Tiur
Jbabhamad
Maran
Al Fruqlos

A
B
Hajjar
C
D

38°E

1

Um At Tababier
Jbab Hannoreh
▲17▲
▲18▲

51
3
Attayas
Palmyra (Tadm

34
Sharifeh
54

Aj'jabbat
Ad Daww

Khan al Hayr
KhanI'hallabat

2
32
⚔ Qasr Al Hayr Al Gharbi
Khar
As's

Wadi al
Rawdah
33

Iadath
Wadi al Luwayzah
85

Hawarin
Al Baridah
Jabal an Niqniqiyeh
Wadi al Mu'ayzil

Al Qaryatein
Khnefees

7

Al Basiri

3
24

Al A'lyaneh

34°N
Bi'r
al 'Ulayyaniyah

Khanl'annabeh
51

Khanl'manqoura
19
Turaq al 'ilab

39▼

10
S y r i a

4
24

Khirbet Al Batmiyat
2
45
As'sabee Byar
Wadi as Sawr

Qasrseiqal
83

Damascus

Wadi Suh Murrah

5

Wadi al Hayl

6
Jabal Siss
▼46▼

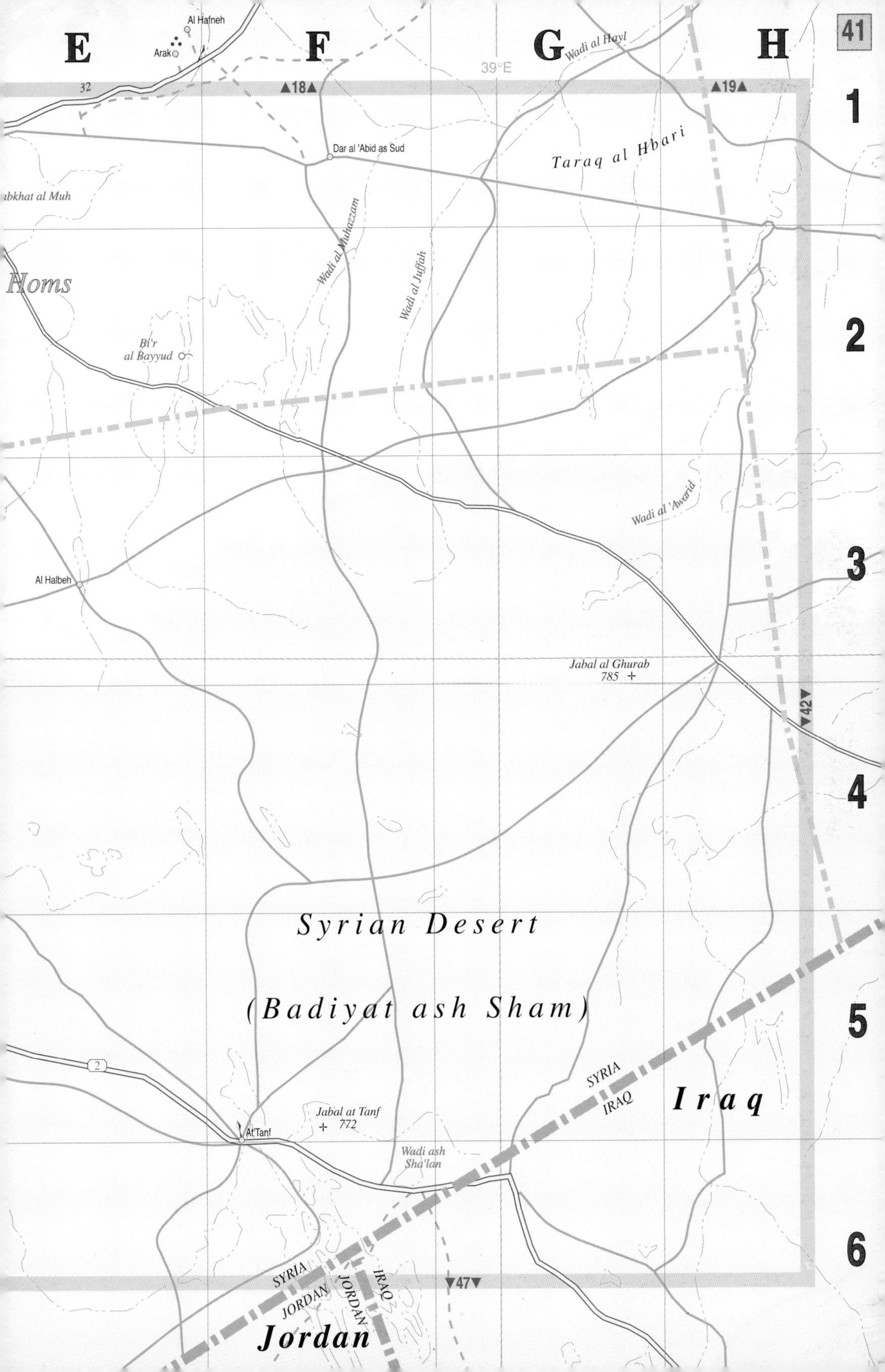

E   F   G   H

1

Al Hafneh

Arak○

▲18▲

39°E

Dar al 'Abid as Sud○

Wadi al Hayl

Taraq al Hbari

▲19▲

Homs

Wadi al Muhazzam

Wadi al Juffah

2

Bi'r
al Bayyud ○

Wadi al 'Awarid

abkhat al Muh

3

Al Halbeh ○

Jabal al Ghurab
785 +

▼42▼

4

S y r i a n   D e s e r t

(B a d i y a t   a s h   S h a m)

5

2

SYRIA

IRAQ

I r a q

Jabal at Tanf
+ 772

At Tanf○

Wadi ash
Sha'lan

6

SYRIA

IRAQ

JORDAN

JORDAN

▼47▼

Jordan

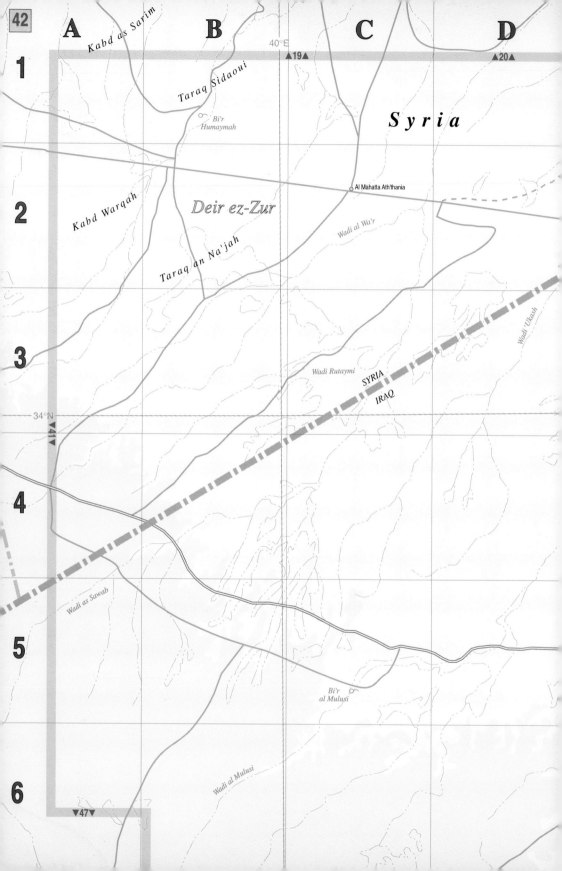

A   B   C   D

1   2   3   4   5   6

40°E

▲19▲   ▲20▲

Kabd as Sarim

Taraq Sidaoui

Bi'r
Humaymah

S y r i a

Al Mahatta Ath'thania

Deir ez-Zur

Kabd Warqah

Wadi al Wa'r

Taraq an Na'jah

Wadi 'Ukash

Wadi Rutaymi

SYRIA

IRAQ

34°N
▼41▼

Wadi as Sawab

Bi'r
al Mulusi

Wadi al Mulusi

▼47▼

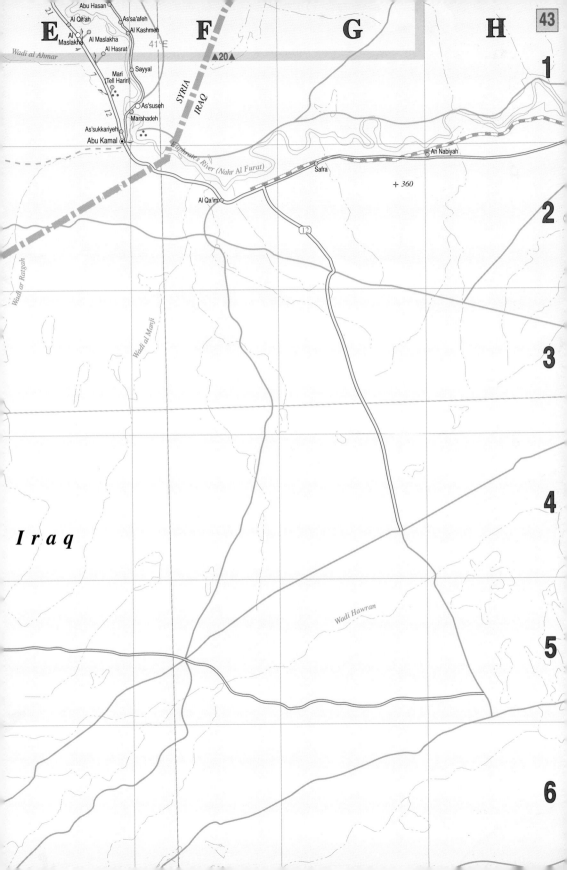

E F G H

1

2

3

4

5

6

Abu Hasan
Al Qit'ah
As'sa'afeh
Al Kashmeh
Al
Maslakha
Al Maslakha
Al Hasrat

Wadi al Ahmar

41°E

▲20▲

Mari
(Tell Hariri)

Sayyal

As'suseh

Marshadeh

As'sukkariyeh

Abu Kamal

SYRIA

IRAQ

Euphrates River (Nahr Al Furat)

Safra

+ 360

An Nabiyah

Al Qa'im

12

Wadi ar Ratgah

Wadi al Manji

I r a q

Wadi Hawran

21

12

7

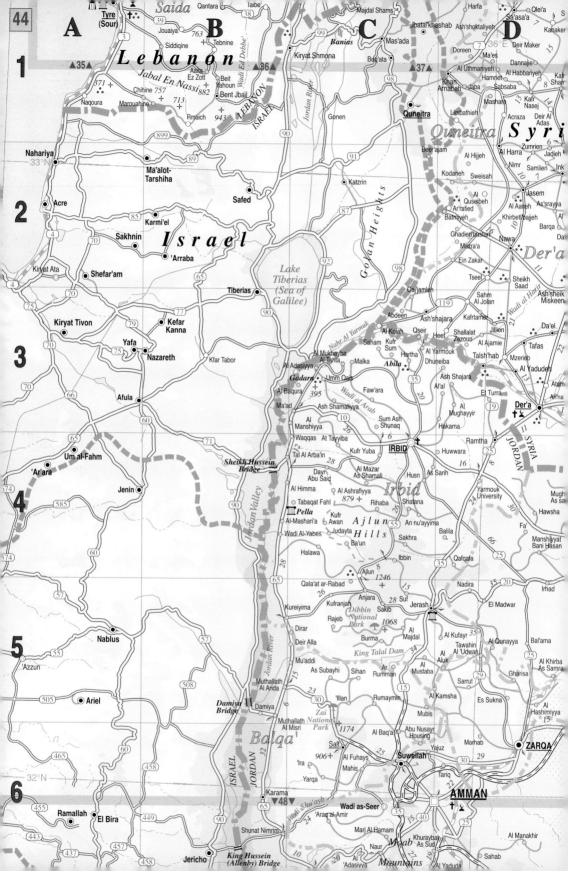

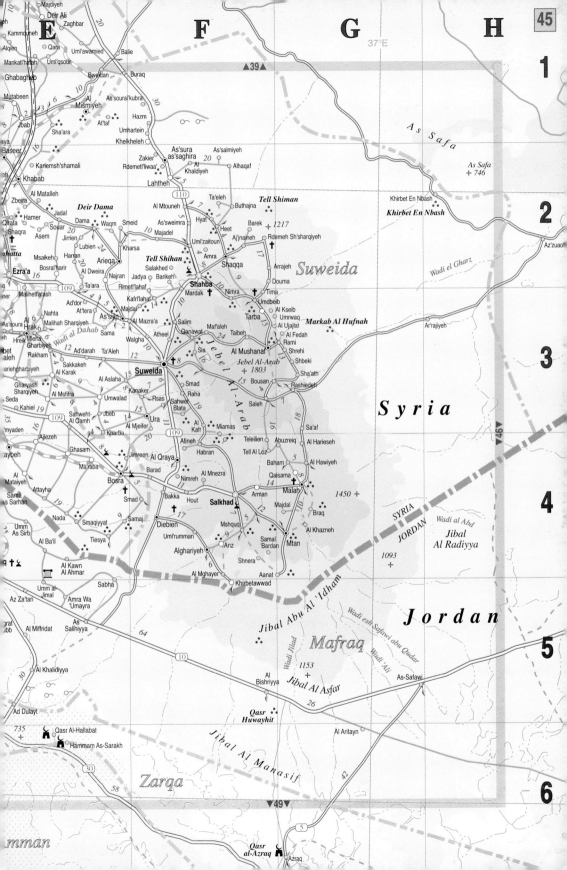

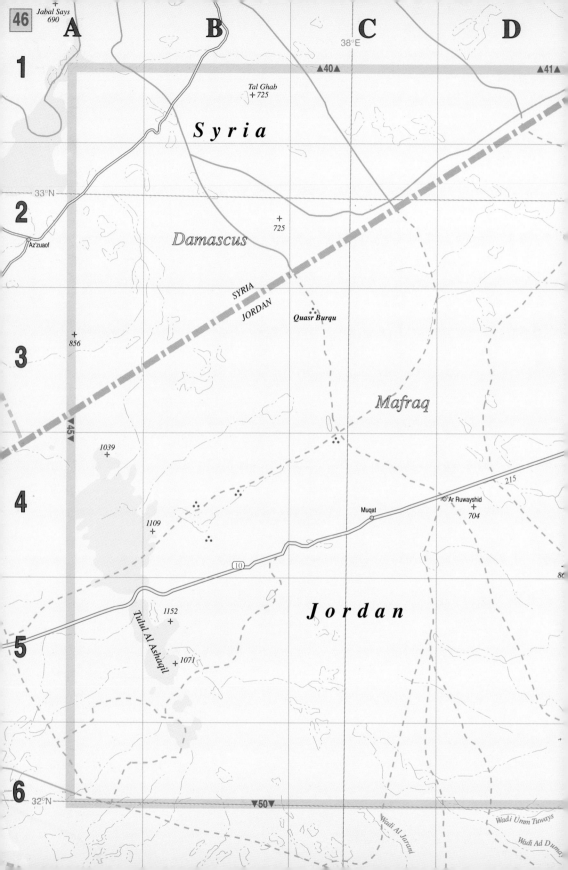

A   **B**   **C**   **D**

1

2

3

4

5

6

Jabal Says
+ 690

▲40▲   38°E

▲41▲

Tal Ghab
+ 725

S y r i a

33°N

+ 725

Damascus

Az'zuaof

SYRIA

JORDAN

Quasr Burqu

+ 856

Mafraq

45▼

1039
+

215

1109
+

Ar Ruwayshid
○

Muqat
○

+ 704

10

J o r d a n

1152
+

Tulul Al Ashaqil

1071
+

86

32°N

▼50▼

Wadi Al Jaráni

Wadi Umm Tuways

Wadi Ad Dumá

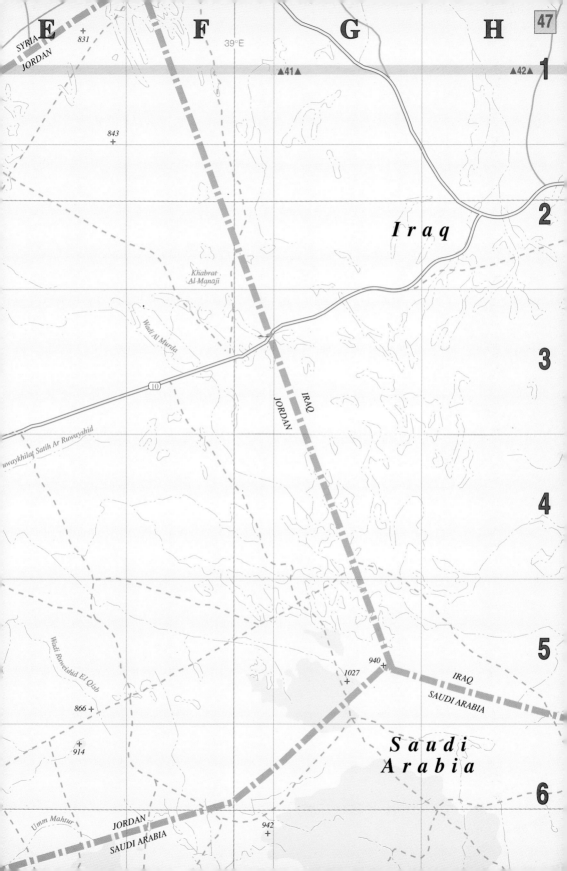

E   + 831   **F**   39°E   **G**   **H**

SYRIA
JORDAN

▲41▲   ▲42▲   **1**

843
+

I r a q   **2**

Khabrat
Al-Manaji

Wadi Al Murda

JORDAN   IRAQ   **3**

10

uwaykhilat Satih Ar Ruwayshid

4

Wadi Ruweishid El Qisb

940
+   **5**
1027
+
IRAQ
SAUDI ARABIA

866 +

S a u d i
A r a b i a

+
914

6

Umm Mahtur   JORDAN
SAUDI ARABIA   942
+

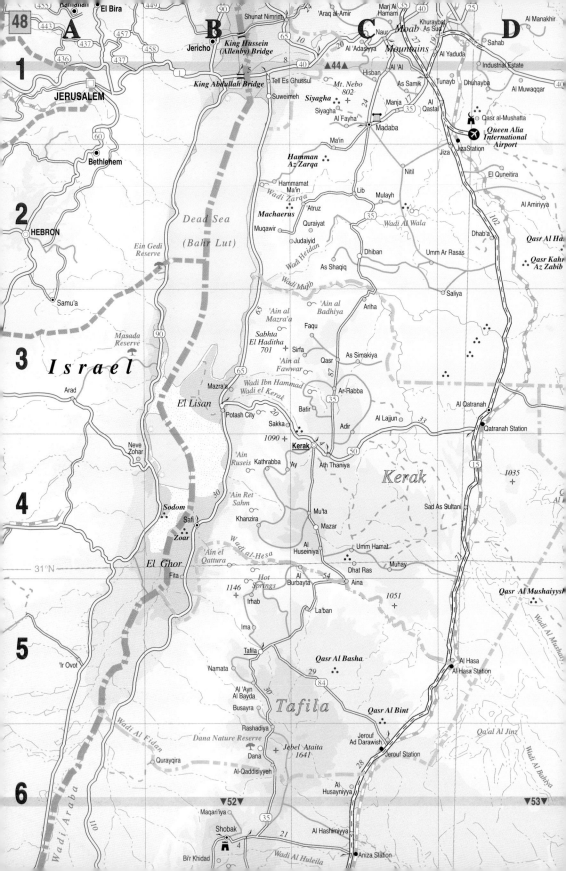

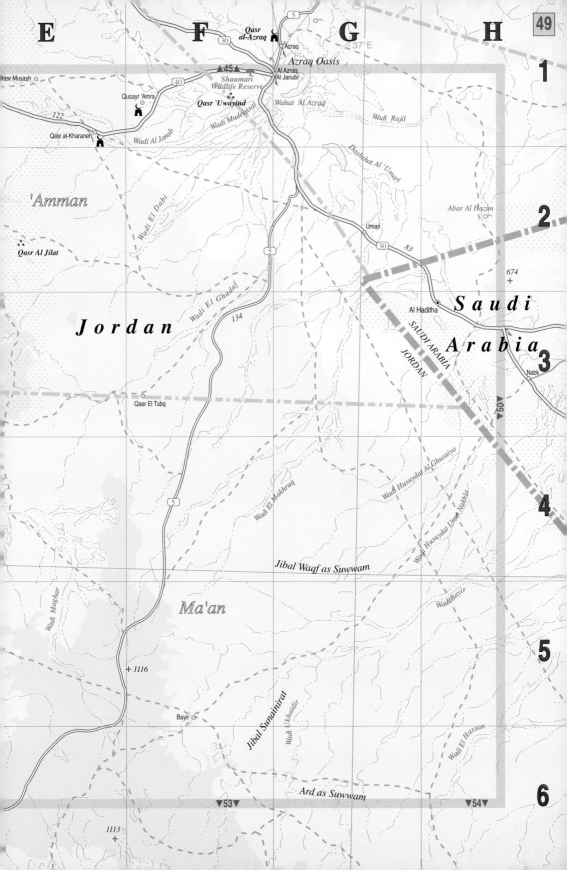

1

2

3

4

5

6

Qasr al-Azraq

Azraq

Azraq Oasis

Al Azraq
Al Janubi

▲45▲

Shaumari
Wildlife Reserve

Qasr 'Uwayind

Wahat Al Azraq

Wadi Rajil

Qasr Musash

Qusayr 'Amra

Wadi Al Janab

Wadi Mudeissat

Dashshat Al 'Umari

Abar Al Hazim

122

Qasr al-Kharaneh

'Amman

Wadi El Dabi

Qasr Al Jilat

Umari

30   83

674
+

S a u d i

Al Haditha

Wadi El Ghadaf

134

J o r d a n

SAUDI ARABIA

JORDAN

A r a b i a

Nabk

▼50▼

Qasr El Tubq

Wadi El Makhruq

Wadi Husuydat Al Ghusaiya

Wadi Husuydat Umm Nakhla

Jibal Waqf as Suwwam

WadiBayir

Ma'an

Wadi Maghar

+ 1116

Jibal Sunainirat

Wadi Ukhaidir

Bayir

Wadi El Hassan

Ard as Suwwam

▼53▼   ▼54▼

1113
+

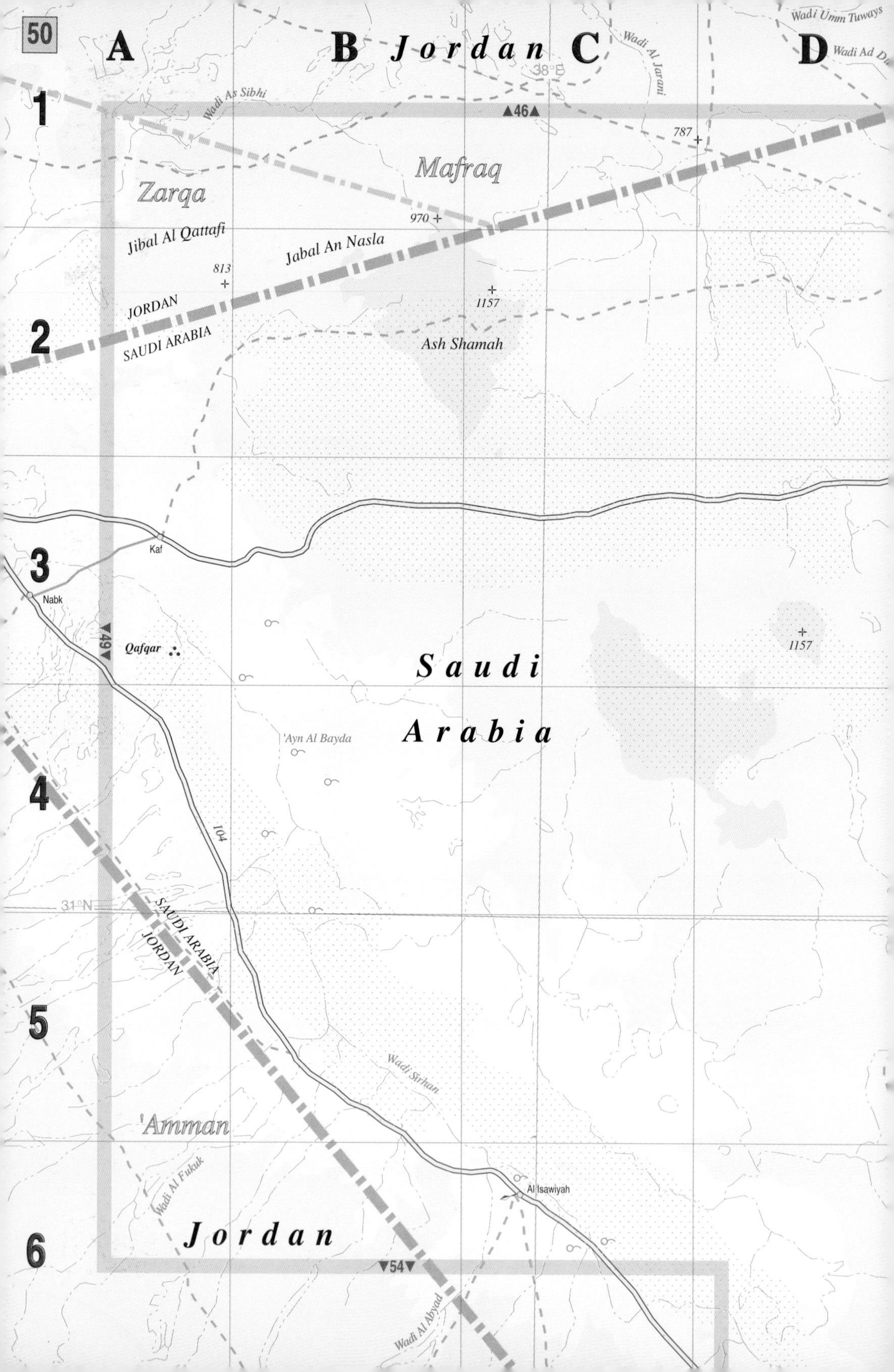

A
D

Wadi Umm Tuways

Wadi Al Jarani

Wadi Ad Di

1

▲46▲

787 +

38°E

Mafraq

Wadi As Sibhi

Zarqa

970 +

Jibal Al Qattafi

Jabal An Nasla

813
+

JORDAN

2

SAUDI ARABIA

1157
+

Ash Shamah

3

Kaf

Nabk

▼49▼

Qafqar .∴

1157
+

S a u d i

'Ayn Al Bayda

A r a b i a

4

104

31°N

SAUDI ARABIA

JORDAN

5

Wadi Sirhan

'Amman

Al Isawiyah

Wadi Al Fuluk

6

J o r d a n

▼54▼

Wadi Al Abyad

Ruins of Aanjar in the Bekaa Valley, Lebanon

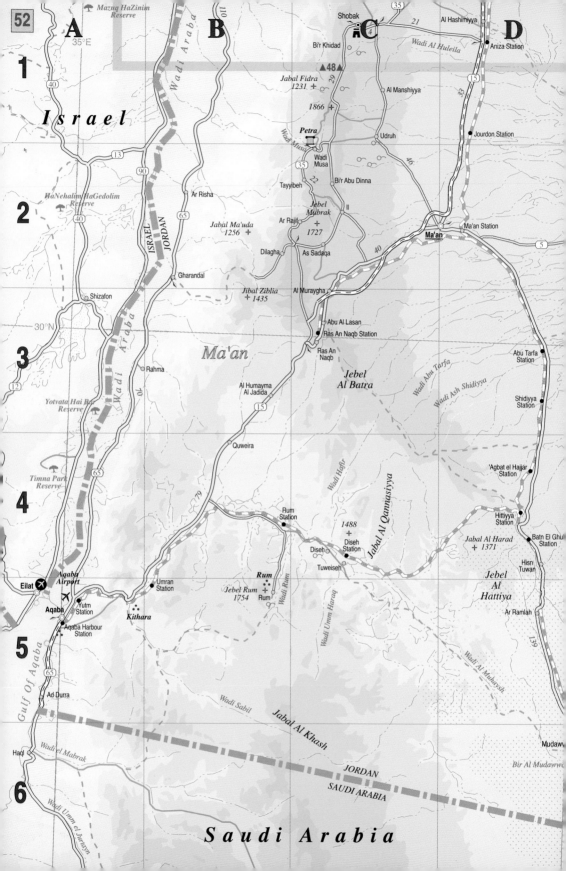

52

A   35°E   B   C   D

1

Mazuq HaZinim Reserve

110

Shobak

Al Hashimiyya

21

Bi'r Khidad

Wadi Al Huleila

Aniza Station

35

▲48▲

29

I s r a e l

Jabal Fidra 1231 +

Al Manshiyya

33

40

13

1866 +

Petra

Udruh

Jourdon Station

15

Wadi Musa

90

65

Wadi Musa

35

2

Ar Risha

Tayyibeh

22

Bi'r Abu Dinna

ISRAEL   *JORDAN*

Jabal Ma'uda 1256 +

Jebel Mubrak

Ar Rajil

1727 +

II

Ma'an

Ma'an Station

46

5

Dilagha

As Sadaqa

40

Gharandal

Al Muraygha

3

Shizafon

Jibal Ziblia + *1435*

Abu Al Lasan

Abu Tarfa Station

30°N

Ma'an

Ras An Naqb Station

Wadi Abu Tarfa

12

Rahma

Ras An Naqb

Jebel Al Batra

Wadi Ash Shidiyya

Shidiyya Station

Al Humayma Al Jadida

15

Yotvata Hai Bar Reserve

'Agbat el Hajjar Station

4

65

79

Quweira

Wadi Hafir

Timna Park Reserve

Rum Station

1488 +

Jabal Al Qamasiyya

Hittiyya Station

Diseh

Diseh Station

Jabal Al Harad + *1371*

Batn El Ghul Station

Aqaba Airport

Tuweiseh

Hisn Tuwan

Eilat

Rum

Wadi Rum

Jebel Al Hattiya

Umran Station

Jebel Rum 1754

Rum

Ar Ramlah

5

Aqaba

Yutm Station

139

Gulf Of Aqaba

Kithara

Aqaba Harbour Station

65

Ad Durra

Wadi Sabil

Jabal Al Khash

Wadi Al Muhaysh

Mudaw

Bir Al Mudawwa

Haql

Wadi el Mabrak

JORDAN

SAUDI ARABIA

6

Wadi Umm el Jurioya

S a u d i   A r a b i a

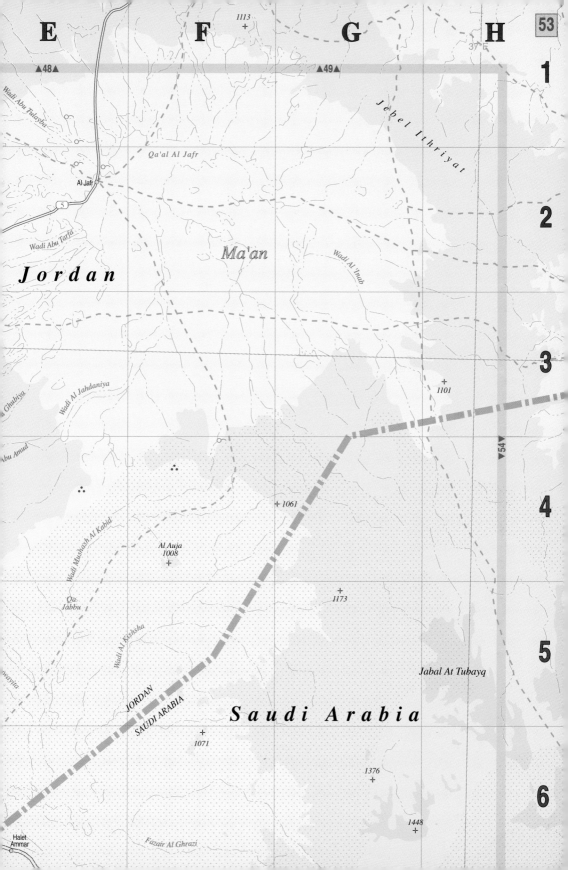

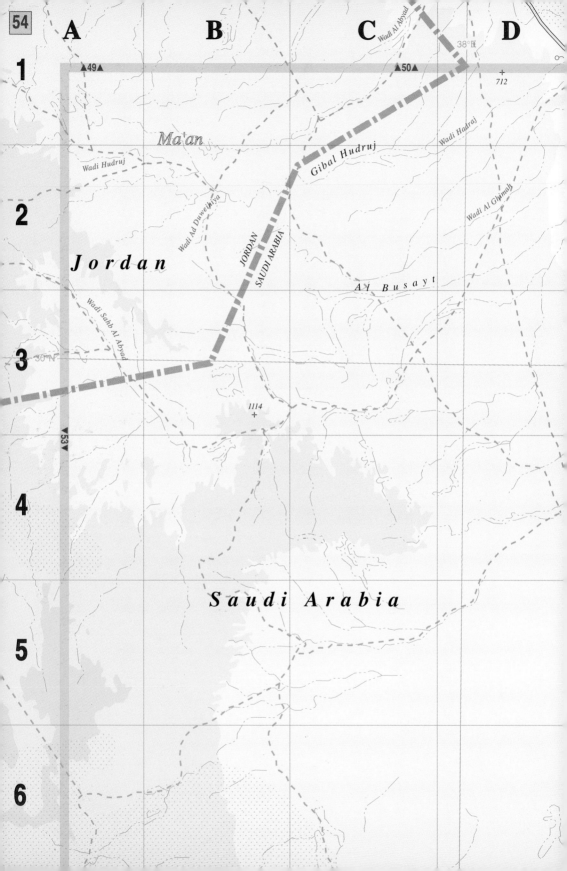

A B C D

1

2

3

4

5

6

Wadi Al Abyad

38°E

▲49▲ ▲50▲ + 712

Ma'an

Wadi Hudruj

Gibal Hudruj

Wadi Hadraj

Wadi Ad Duweihiya

JORDAN SAUDI ARABIA

Wadi Al Ghimah

Jordan

Al Busayt

Wadi Sahb Al Abyad

30°N

1114 +

▼53▼

Saudi Arabia

Getting Around Jordan, Syria & Lebanon

Bus

Jordan The most comfortable way to travel is with the enormous blue-and-white JETT buses that serve all the main Jordan tourist routes. It is important to book two days in advance though as they get heavily booked up. Smaller, private buses serve just about every destination you can think of.

The smaller towns are served by 20-seat minibuses which leave when full. Fares are cheap although you may have to pay the fare for the full journey even if you are not going to the end of the line. It's a good idea to establish the fare before taking the ride. You can hail these buses at any point along the route and, generally, they will pick you up if they are not already full.

Syria There are four levels of bus service operating in Syria, with four levels of price to match. The most expensive and comfortable are the 'luxury' buses – operators include Qadmous, Al-Ahliah and Al-Ryan. Tickets must be booked in advance (owing to demand) and these buses leave according to a timetable – on the dot.

The government-owned Karnak bus service was once considered the deluxe carrier of the Syrian highways, but now with so many rival companies employing faster, sleeker vehicles, Karnak looks a poor cousin by comparison. That said, they are perfectly good and somewhat cheaper than luxury buses. You must always buy a ticket, with seat assigned, prior to boarding. Karnak buses usually have stations in the centre of towns, while the luxury bus companies on occasion require a little more effort to track down.

A similar service is offered by the Pullman bus company. Pullmans are semi-private and run to a set timetable, but are often rather clapped-out and slow. They also have a booking system but the demand is not so great. Pullman buses are marginally cheaper than Karnak buses but not as cheap as the funky local buses.

Microbuses (locally referred to as *meecros*) are modern vans that have been adapted to squeeze in a few more people. These are used principally on short hops between cities and many routes to small towns and villages. They are generally expensive and leave when full, but because they are smaller and there is no standing room departures are considerably more frequent.

At the bottom rung of the road transport ladder are buses and minibuses of a hard-to-determine vintage that formed the bulk of Syria's public bus system until the end of the 1980s. The buses are far less comfortable than the more modern alternatives but as the distances are short it's no real hardship and it's one of the best ways to meet local people. Buses connect to all major towns, while the minibus variety work on short hops and serve more out-of-the-way places. Minibuses look fairly plain from the outside but inside they are decorated with an extraordinary array of gaudy ornaments. They have no schedule and leave

ANN JOUSIFFE

Street market in Amman, Jordan

when they are full. Journey times are generally longer than those of other buses as they set people down and pick them up at any point along the route, hence their nickname of *stop-stops* among the locals. Fares are cheap, although often you will be charged marginally more on minibuses which cover the same route as their bigger brothers.

Caution: It can be considered offensive for men to sit next to women on the buses – at least more elderly and conservative women. If, when boarding, a male traveller only finds free seats next to local women, it would be prudent to remain standing. Often passengers will rearrange themselves so that women sit together, or with family members, and free up the spare seats. If a male traveller does sit down next to a local woman and people get animated, the best advice is not to argue about it.

Lebanon The civil war put paid to the public bus service but gradually things are improving. There are now buses serving all the main routes around Beirut, including the airport. They have a low, fixed fare and operate a 'hail and ride' system. There are also buses serving the main towns in the country, although they do not operate to a fixed timetable.

Train

Jordan A weekly train connects Amman with Damascus along the old Hejaz railway line. The remaining lines are used exclusively by goods trains.

Syria There is a passenger service between Damascus and Qamishle via Aleppo, Deir ez-Zur and Hassake. Trains also operate on a couple of secondary lines, one of which runs from Aleppo to Lattakia, and then along the coast to Tartus and on to Homs and Damas-

cus. The Hejaz railway, which originally ran from Damascus to Medina in Saudi Arabia, ferrying pilgrims to Mecca, still has a small part of its line up and running – twice a week a slow diesel train (or if train buffs are in luck, a steam train) runs from Damascus to Der'a. One of these continues to Amman in Jordan. In summer trains run along the Barada Valley.

Syrian trains are cheap and sometimes punctual but there are never more than three services a day between any given destinations, often fewer. Worse, the stations are usually awkwardly located a few kilometres from the centre of town, so that unless you are particularly enamoured of trains you are better off with the more practical buses and service taxis. First class is air-con with aircraft-type seats; 2nd class is the same without air-con. Sleepers (*manaama*) are also available.

Lebanon In Lebanon there are no passenger services still running and much of the old track has been ripped up, blown up or built over, so there is not much chance of the railway being restored. There are plans, however, to build a new line from Beirut to Damascus.

Service Taxi

Jordan Service taxis serve on many routes and leave when full. They usually fill up quickly as they only have five or seven seats. They cost up to twice as much as the minibuses but are faster as they stop less along the way to pick up or set down passengers.

Syria This country has a system of service taxis (*servees*) which only operate along the most popular routes. They cost about three times as much as buses but have the advantage of being faster and, having only five passenger seats, fill up more quickly.

Lebanon This country has service taxis and taxis which are recognisable by their red number plates. Service taxis usually follow a preset route and you can stop them anywhere by saying 'indak' (here) to the driver. You may have to take more than one service taxi if your destination is not on one of the driver's preset routes. Until recently service taxis were the only way of getting around and they are still a favourite option. The fares are cheap and you seldom have to wait long to hail one down.

Ordinary taxis are not confined to a set route and take only one fare. You can order taxis by telephone.

Often cars will stop for you which are not official taxis but freelancers. If you choose to take a ride from one of these be sure to agree on a fare beforehand.

Road

Jordan There is no problem bringing your own vehicle into Jordan, although you will need a carnet de passage en douane and your own insurance. The UK Automobile Association requires a financial guarantee for the carnet, which effectively acts as an import duty waiver. It is essential to fill out the carnet properly at each border or you could be asked for a lot of money when you leave the country.

The road system is generally good and the driving not too erratic by Middle Eastern standards. Vehicles are driven on the right-hand side of the road and most places you're likely to be heading for are signposted in English as well as Arabic. On the open road the general speed limit is 90 kmh and on the Desert Highway 110 kmh.

Cars can be hired in Jordan quite easily although hire charges are a bit high. If you want to explore the desert regions such as Wadi Rum, a good 4WD is essential.

Syria As with Jordan you will need a carnet de passage if you bring your own car or motorbike. In addition you will need your vehicle registration papers and an International Driving Permit. Third-party insurance must be bought at the border at the rate of US$36 a month. Its value is questionable and it is worth making sure that your own insurance covers you for Syria, especially as some Middle Eastern countries are considered 'war zones'. Long-distance night driving can be hazardous, as not all drivers believe in using headlights all the time.

You can hire a car in Syria although the choice can be a bit limited and it is not cheap. It is well worth considering though if there is more than one person and you are planning to visit some of the less accessible places.

Lebanon There are plenty of car-hire firms in Lebanon and prices are competitive. The main problem is the hazardous traffic conditions. Accidents and traffic jams are frequent, especially in Beirut and on the busy coastal road. Inland the terrain is mountainous with twisting, narrow roads. In winter some of these roads are closed. If you intend to take your own vehicle it is important to check with a Lebanese embassy about import duties as they can be prohibitively high.

Bicycle

Jordan Cycling is a possibility in Jordan but not necessarily a fun one. The intense heat of the summer can cause heatstroke and dehydration if you are not careful. Cycling north or south (the orientation of most routes) can be hard work too. There's a strong prevailing wind from the west that can wear you down. Bring plenty of spare parts.

Syria Few people cycle in Syria as the climate does not encourage it, especially in summer. The heat is too great and so are the distances. Still, if you're determined to cycle then there is nothing to stop you – make sure you take plenty of spares as they will be hard to get locally.

Lebanon Traffic conditions make cycling extremely hazardous on the main roads, if not downright suicidal. The mountain areas are ideal for cycling if you have a mountain bike, but be warned: the terrain is extremely rugged and you need to be very fit to tackle the mountain roads. Once again it would be a good idea to take plenty of spares with you.

PETER & ANN JOUSIFFE

Entrance to the citadel, Aleppo, Syria

Comment Circuler en Jordanie, en Syrie et au Liban

Bus

Jordanie Les énormes bus JETT bleus et blancs, qui desservent les principaux itinéraires touristiques du pays, sont le moyen de transport le plus confortable. Les places à bord étant très prisées, il est préférable de réserver deux jours à l'avance. Des bus privés plus petits se rendent vers toutes les destinations possibles.

La majorité des villes sont desservies par des minibus de 20 places, qui partent quand ils sont complets. Les tarifs sont bon marché, mais il se peut que vous deviez payer pour tout le trajet desservi, même si vous vous arrêtez en chemin. Se mettre d'accord sur le prix du voyage avant de partir peut parfois s'avérer utile. On peut héler ce bus à n'importe quel point de leur parcours et, en règle générale, ils vous prendront, à moins qu'ils ne soient déjà complets.

Syrie Le pays dispose de quatre catégories de bus, correspondant à quatre catégories de prix. Les plus onéreux et les plus confortables sont les bus "de luxe" que proposent par

exemple les compagnies Qadmous, Al-Ahliah et Al-Ryan. En raison d'une forte demande, il faut réserver sa place. Ces bus suivent un horaire et sont très ponctuels.

Le service public de bus Karnak, autrefois considéré comme la compagnie de luxe, fait maintenant figure de parent pauvre, en raison de la concurrence des compagnies privées qui utilisent des véhicules plus rapides et mieux entretenus. Cela étant dit, ils sont tout à fait corrects et passablement moins chers que les bus de luxe. Il est nécessaire d'acheter son billet, comportant un numéro de place, avant le départ. Les bus Karnak disposent généralement d'arrêts en centre-ville, alors que les compagnies d'autobus de luxe sont parfois moins faciles à localiser.

La compagnie de bus Pullman propose un service équivalent. Il s'agit d'une compagnie semi-privée qui suit des horaires fixes, mais ses véhicules sont souvent fatigués et lents. Ils disposent d'un système de réservation mais les demandes ne sont pas très nombreuses.

Les bus Pullman sont légèrement moins chers que les bus Karnak, mais moins bon marché que les pittoresques bus locaux.

Les "microbus" (appelés meecros) sont des camionnettes modernes, modifiées afin de pouvoir accueillir quelques passagers supplémentaires. Principalement employés pour de courts trajets de ville à ville, ils desservent de nombreuses petites localités et villages. Ils reviennent généralement cher et ne partent que lorsqu'ils sont complets. Heureusement ils sont petits et ne disposent pas de places debout, ce qui augmente la fréquence des départs.

Au dernier échelon du transport routier, se trouvent les bus et minibus de marque et d'année indéterminées qui constituaient l'essentiel du transport public syrien jusqu'à la fin des années 80. S'ils sont beaucoup moins confortables que leurs parents plus modernes, ils ne présentent pas une épreuve insurmontable car les distances sont peu importantes. Les bus relient les principales villes, tandis que les minibus sont réservés aux dis-

Port of the ancient city of Byblos (Jbail), Lebanon

PETER JOUSIFFE

tances courtes et aux destinations peu fréquentées. Ils n'ont pas d'horaires et se contentent de partir lorsqu'ils sont pleins. De plus, ils sont généralement lents car ils s'arrêtent pour laisser monter ou descendre les voyageurs où ceux-ci le désirent, ce qui explique leur surnom local de stop-stop. Les tarifs sont peu élevés, bien que les minibus soient relativement plus chers que les bus sur un même trajet.

Attention ! Tant en Syrie qu'en Jordanie, le fait pour un homme de s'asseoir près d'une femme dans un bus – à plus forte raison s'il s'agit d'une femme d'un certain âge ou de mœurs traditionnelles – peut être considéré comme offensant. Si un passager, en montant dans le bus, constate que les sièges libres sont tous à côté de femmes, il doit rester debout. Souvent les passagers changeront de place, afin que les femmes soient assises ensemble ou près de membres de leur famille, libérant ainsi des sièges. En tout cas, si un homme s'assoit à côté d'une femme et que les gens protestent, la meilleure attitude est de ne pas répliquer.

Liban La guerre civile a perturbé le service de bus publics mais, petit à petit, la situation s'améliore. Il y a maintenant des bus qui desservent tous les principaux parcours aux alentours de Beyrouth, notamment l'aéroport. Leur tarif unique est peu élevé et, pour les prendre, il suffit de faire signe au machiniste. Il existe également de bus qui desservent les principales villes provinciales mais ils ne circulent pas selon un horaire fixe.

Train

Jordanie En Jordanie, un train hebdomadaire relie Amman à Damas par la vieille ligne de chemin de fer du Hedjaz. Les autres lignes sont réservées uniquement aux trains de marchandises.

Syrie Un train de voyageurs relie Damas à Qamishle, via Alep, Deir ez-Zur et Hassake. Des trains circulent aussi sur deux lignes secondaires, l'une entre Alep et Lattaquié et l'autre le long de la côte, vers Tartous, Homs et Damas. Un troncon de la ligne du Hedjaz (qui, à l'origine, allait de Damas à Médine en Arabie Saoudite, transportant des pèlerins à destination de la Mecque) fonctionne toujours – deux fois par semaine, un omnibus tracté par une locomotive diesel (ou, si les amateurs de trains ont de la chance, un train à vapeur) fait le trajet de Damas à Deraa. L'un d'eux continue jusqu'à Amman, en Jordanie. En été, les trains longent la vallée de la Barada.

Les trains syriens sont bon marché et parfois à l'heure, mais n'offrent jamais plus de trois liaisons quotidiennes vers une destination donnée (et souvent moins). Autre inconvénient : les gares se trouvent souvent à plusieurs kilomètres du centre-ville. A moins d'être un passionné du rail, mieux vaut donc emprunter les bus ou les taxis-service. La première classe ferroviaire est équipée de la climatisation et de sièges d'un confort comparable à ceux que l'on trouve à bord des avions de ligne. La seconde classe est comparable, l'air conditionné en moins. Des voitures-couchettes (*manaama*) sont également disponibles.

Liban Plus aucun train de voyageurs ne circule au Liban, une grande partie des voies qui existaient ayant été arrachée, bombardée ou remplacée par de nouvelles constructions. Les chances sont donc maigres de voir restaurer le réseau ferroviaire, bien que la construction d'une nouvelle ligne entre Beyrouth et Damas soit en cours d'étude.

Taxis-service

Jordanie Les taxis-service, qui desservent de nombreux itinéraires, partent dès qu'ils sont complets. Ils le sont généralement assez vite puisqu'ils ont une capacité de cinq à sept sièges. Leur coût est deux fois plus élevé que celui des minibus mais ils sont plus rapides, puisqu'ils s'arrêtent moins en cours de route pour prendre ou déposer des passagers.

Syrie Le pays possède un réseau de taxis-service (servees) qui ne desservent que les itinéraires les plus fréquentes. Ils reviennent trois fois plus cher que les bus, mais ils ont l'avantage d'être plus rapides et de se remplir plus vite.

Liban Le Liban dispose de taxis-service et de taxis ordinaires, reconnaissables à leurs plaques d'immatriculation rouges. Les taxis-service suivent généralement un itinéraire préétabli et s'arrêtent où vous le souhaitez : il suffit de dire indak (ici) au conducteur. Il se peut que vous deviez changer de taxi si votre destination n'est pas sur l'itinéraire du conducteur. Seul moyen de déplacement jusqu'à une période récente, les taxis-service restent un moyen de transport apprécié. Les tarifs sont bas et il est rare de devoir attendre longtemps pour en obtenir un.

Les taxis ordinaires, qu'il est possible de commander par téléphone, ne se limitent pas à un itinéraire et ne prennent qu'un client à la fois.

Souvent, vous verrez s'arrêter des voitures qui ne sont pas des taxis officiels mais des indépendants. Si vous décidez d'avoir recours à leurs services, n'oubliez surtout pas de vous mettre d'accord sur le prix avant le départ.

Route

Jordanie Venir en Jordanie avec votre véhicule ne pose

aucun problème, vous aurez seulement besoin d'un carnet de passage en douane et de votre assurance automobile. La UK Automobile Association exige une garantie financière pour le carnet, car il dispense du versement de droits à l'importation. Assurez-vous que le carnet est correctement rempli à chaque frontière, sans quoi vous pourriez être soumis à des taxes importantes en quittant le pays.

Le réseau routier est relativement bon et la conduite, à droite, est assez raisonnable selon les critères moyen-orientaux. De nombreuses destinations sont indiquées en anglais et en arabe. Sur route, la vitesse est généralement limitée a 90 km/h, sauf sur la Desert Highway, où elle atteint 110 km/h.

Il est très facile de louer un véhicule en Jordanie, mais le coût de location est relativement élevé. Si vous désirez explorer les régions désertiques comme le Wadi Rum, il est essentiel de conduire un bon 4x4.

Syrie Tout comme en Jordanie, il vous faudra un carnet de passage si vous arrivez avec votre voiture ou votre moto. En outre, vous devrez présenter les papiers d'immatriculation du véhicule et un permis de conduire international. Une assurance responsabilité civile, d'un montant de 36 $US par mois, doit être souscrite à la frontière. La protection qu'elle offre étant discutable, mieux vaut vous assurer que votre police habituelle couvre la Syrie, d'autant plus que certains pays du Moyen-Orient sont souvent considérés comme des régions en guerre. Il peut être dangereux de parcourir de longs trajets de nuit, les conducteurs n'estimant pas tous nécessaire d'allumer leurs phares.

S'il est possible de louer une voiture en Syrie, le choix est un peu limité et les prix assez élevés. C'est pourtant une

Temple of Bel, Palmyra (Tadmor), Syria

PETER AND ANN JOUSIFFE

bonne solution si vous voyagez à plusieurs et que vous projetez de visiter des endroits isolés.

Liban Les nombreuses entreprises de location de voitures au Liban offrent des prix compétitifs. Les conditions de conduite, dangereuses, restent la principale source de problèmes. Les accidents et les embouteillages sont fréquents, notamment dans Beyrouth et sur la route côtière. Les routes de l'intérieur du pays, montagneux, sont étroites et tortueuses. Certaines sont fermées en hiver. Si vous envisagez de prendre votre propre véhicule, pensez à demander auprès de l'ambassade du Liban quels sont les droits d'importation : ils peuvent se révéler prohibitifs.

Bicyclette

Jordanie La bicyclette n'est sans doute pas le moyen de transport le plus agréable pour parcourir la Jordanie. En été, la chaleur intense peut provoquer insolations et déshydratation si vous n'êtes pas prudent. Le

voyage vers le nord ou le sud (la plupart des routes sont orientées ainsi) est parfois rendu difficile par le fort vent d'ouest dominant qui peut même vous jeter au sol. Pensez à prendre beaucoup de pièces de rechange.

Syrie Rares sont les cyclistes en Syrie : la chaleur est trop forte et les distances sont longues. Mais si vous en avez décidé ainsi, rien ne vous arrêtera. Assurez-vous seulement d'emporter toutes les pièces de rechange nécessaires, elles seraient difficiles à obtenir sur place.

Liban En raison des conditions de circulation, il est extrêmement dangereux, voire suicidaire, d'emprunter les routes principales à bicyclette. Les zones montagneuses sont idéales pour les VTT, mais le terrain est très accidenté et il faut être bien entraîné pour venir à bout des routes de montagne. Encore une fois, n'oubliez surtout pas d'emporter de nombreuses pièces de rechange.

Reisen in Jordanien, Syrien und im Libanon

Bus

Jordanien Am bequemsten reist man mit den riesigen blau-weißen JETT Bussen, welche die wichtigsten Touristenstrecken in Jordanien bedienen. Es ist wichtig, zwei Tage im voraus zu buchen, da sie schnell ausgebucht sind. Kleinere, private Busse bedienen so ziemlich jedes Reiseziel, das man sich vorstellen kann.

Kleinere Orte werden von 20-Sitzer Minibussen bedient, die abfahren, sobald sie voll sind.

Die Fahrpreise sind billig, obwohl man eventuell den Preis für die Gesamtstrecke zahlen muß, auch wenn man gar nicht bis zur Endstation fährt. Es empfiehlt sich, den Preis vor Fahrtantritt festzulegen. Man kann diese Busse an beliebiger Stelle entlang der Route herbeiwinken und im allgemeinem wenn sie nicht voll besitzt sind, nehmen sie einen mit.

Syrien In Syrien gibt es vier Stufen von Busdiensten mit den entsprechenden Preiskategorien.

Die teuersten und komfortabelsten sind die "Luxus"-Busse – darunter Unternehmen wie Quadmous, Al-Ahliah und Al-Ryan. Die Fahrkarten müssen (wegen der Nachfrage) im Voraus gelöst werden. Und diese Busse fahren nach Fahrplan, pünktlich auf die Minute.

Der staatseigene Karnak Busdienst galt einst als der Luxustransporter der Syrischen Hauptverkehrsstraßen. Heute jedoch, wo so viele Konkurrenzunternehmen schnellere, schnittigere Fahrzeuge einsetzen, wirkt Karnak im Vergleich eher ärmlich. Aber sie sind in Ordnung and etwas billiger als die "Luxus"-Busse. Grundsätzlich muß man die Fahrkarte, mit Platznumerierung, vor dem Einsteigen lösen. Karnak Busse haben normaler-

weise Büros in Stadtzentrum, während die Büros der "Luxus"-Busse manchmal schwierige zu finden sind.

Ein ähnlicher Service wird vom Busunternehmen Pullman angeboten. Pullmans sind zur Hälfte privatisiert und fahren nach Fahrplan. Sie sind allerdings oft schon schrottreif und langsam. Auch hier gibt es ein Buchungssystem, allerdings ist die Nachfrage nicht so groß. Pullman Busse sind geringfügig billiger als die Karnak Busse aber nicht so billig wie die poppigen lokalen Busse.

Mikrobusse (vor Ort als *Meekros* bezeichnet) sind moderne Lieferwagen, die umgebaut wurden um ein paar mehr Leute hineinzuquetschen. Sie werden hauptsächlich auf Kurzstrecken zwischen den Städten und auf vielen Strecken zu kleinen Städten und Ortschaften eingesetzt. Im allgemeinen sind die Mikrobusse teuer und fahren los, sobald sie voll sind. Da sie kleiner sind und keine Stehplätze haben, sind die Abfahrten bedeutend häufiger.

Auf der untersten Stufe stehen die Busse und Minibusse von schwer definierbarem Baujahr, welche bis Ende der 80er die Masse des öffentlichen Busnetzes in Syrien ausgemacht haben. Diese Busse sind we-

sentlich unbequemer als die moderneren Alternativen, doch bei den kurzen Entfernungen kann man es aushalten. Dafür bieten sie eine der besten Wege, die Einheimischen kennenzulernen. Alle wichtigen Städte werden durch Busse verbunden, während die Minibus-Variante auf den Kurzstecken verkehrt und die abgelegenen Orte bedient. Von außen sehen die Minibusse ziemlich schlicht aus. Im Inneren sind sie jedoch mit einem ausgefallenen Mix farbenprächtiger Ornamente dekoriert. Sie haben keinen Fahrplan und fahren ab, sobald sie voll sind. Die Fahrtzeiten sind im Allgemeinen länger als bei anderen Bussen, da Fahrgäste entlang der Strecke beliebig aus- und einsteigen können. Deshalb auch der Spitzname *Stop-Stops* unter den Einheimischen. Fahrpreise sind billig, auch wenn man oft minimal mehr bei Minibussen bezahlen muß, welche die gleiche Strecke wie ihre großen Brüder befahren.

Achtung: Es kann als anstößig angesehen werden, wenn Männer im Bus neben Frauen sitzen – zumindest bei älteren und konservativeren Frauen. Wenn ein männlicher Reisender beim Einsteigen nur noch freie Plätze neben

ANN JOUSIFFE

Facade of the monastery at Petra, Jordan

einheimischen Frauen findet, sollte er klugerweise stehenbleiben. Die Fahrgäste werden sich oft so umsetzen, daß Frauen nebeneinander oder bei Familienmitgliedern sitzen, um die Sitzplätze freizumachen. Wenn sich ein männlicher Reisender doch neben eine einheimische Frau setzt und die Leute lebhaft werden, ist es am besten, sich nicht auf eine Diskussion einzulassen.

Libanon Der Burgerkrieg hat dem öffentlichen Busverkehr ein Ende gesetzt aber die Lage verbessert sich allmählich, und neue Dienste machen ständig auf. Es gibt jetzt Busse auf allen Hauptverkehrsstrecken um Beirut herum, wie auch zum Flughafen. Die Fahrpreise sind niedrig und festgesetzt, und man winkt die Busse herbei. Busse fahren auch zwischen allen größeren Städten im Land.

Zug
Jordanien In Jordanien, ein wöchentlicher Zug verbindet Amman und Damaskus entlang der alten Hejaz Eisenbahnlinie. Die anderen Linien werden ausschließlich von Güterzügen benutzt.

Syrien Es gibt einen Passagierzug zwischen Damaskus und Quamishle über Aleppo, Deir ez-Zur und Hassake. Züge verkehren auch auf einigen Nebenstrecken. Eine führt von Aleppo nach Lattakia und dann entlang der Küste nach Tartus und weiter nach Homs und Damaskus. Die Hejaz Eisenbahnlinie, die ursprünglich von Damaskus nach Medina in Saudi-Arabien führte und Pilger nach Mekka brachte, wird immer noch auf einem kleinen Teilstück befahren. Zweimal in der Woche gibt es einen langsamen Dieselzug (oder, wenn man Gluck hat, ein Dampfzug) von Damaskus nach Der'a. Einer der beiden Züge fährt

weiter nach Amman in Jordanien. Im Sommer gibt es Züge durch das Barada Tal.

Züge in Syrien sind billig und manchmal pünktlich. Allerdings gibt es nie mehr als drei Verbindungen am Tag zwischen den einzelnen Zielen, oft noch weniger. Schlimmer noch, die Bahnhöfe sind im Allgemeinen ungünstig einige Kilometer außerhalb des Stadtzentrums gelegen, so daß man mit den praktischeren Bussen und Servicetaxis besser dran ist. Es sei denn, man hat ein besonderes Faible für die Eisenbahn. Die Erste Klasse ist mit Klimaanlage und Flugzeugähnlichen Sitzen ausgestattet. Zweite Klasse ebenso aber ohne Klimaanlage. Schlafwagen (*manaama*) sind auch erhältlich.

Libanon Im Libanon gibt es keinen Passagierverkehr mehr und viel von der alten Strecke wurde aufgerissen, gesprengt oder überbaut. Daher besteht wohl kaum eine Chance, daß die alte Eisenbahnstecke wiederaufgebaut wird. Es existieren allerdings Pläne, eine neue Linie von Beirut nach Damaskus zu bauen.

Servicetaxi
Jordan Servicetaxis bedienen viele Strecken und fahren los, sobald sie voll sind. Im Allgemeinen füllen sie sich schnell, da sie nur fünf oder sieben Sitze haben. Sie kosten bis zu doppelt soviel wie die Minibusse, sind aber schneller, da sie weniger entlang der Strecke anhalten, um Fahrgäste ein- oder aussteigen zu lassen.

Syrien In Syrien gibt es ein Servicetaxi-Netz (*servees*), welches nur entlang der beliebtesten Strecken operiert. Servicetaxis kosten ungefähr das Dreifache der Busse, haben aber den Vorteil, schneller zu sein und sich rascher zu füllen, da sie nur fünf Passagiersitze haben.

Libanon Im Libanon gibt es Servicetaxis und Taxis, welche an ihren roten Nummernschildern erkennbar sind. Servicetaxis folgen normalerweise einer festen Route. Man kann sie überall anhalten, indem man "indak" (hier) zum Fahrer sagt. Eventuell muß man mehrere Servicetaxis nehmen, wenn das Ziel nicht auf der Fahrtstrecke eines Fahrers liegt. Bis vor kurzem waren die Servicetaxis das einzige Verkehrsmittel und sie sind immer noch eine beliebte Wahl. Die Fahrpreise sind billig und man muß selten lange warten, bis eines anhält.

Normale Taxis sind nicht auf bestimmte Routen beschränkt und nehmen nur eine Fuhre mit. Taxis können per Telefon bestellt werden.

Häufig halten Autos an, die keine offiziellen Taxis sondern Freelancers sind. Wenn man eines von diesen für eine Fahrt auswählt, sollte man den Fahrpreis im voraus aushandeln.

Straße
Jordanien Man kann problemlos das eigene Auto nach Jordanien mitbringen. Allerdings benötigt man einen Zollpassierschein und eine eigene Versicherung. Die britische Automobilvereinigung verlangt eine finanzielle Garantie für den Zollpassierschein, der wie eine Importzoll Verzichtserklärung fungiert. Es ist wichtig, sicherzustellen, daß der Zollpassierschein an jeder Grenze korrekt ausgefüllt wird, da es sonst beim Verlassen des Landes teuer werden kann.

Das Straßennetz ist im Allgemeinen gut und das Fahren ist nach Maßstab des Nahen Ostens nicht zu unberechenbar. Es herrscht Rechtsverkehr und die meisten Orte, die man wohl anfährt, sind in Arabisch und Englisch ausgeschildert. Auf der Landstraße ist die Geschwindigkeitsbegrenzung 90 km/h, auf der Wüsten Fernstraße 110 km/h.

Man kann in Jordanien ziemlich einfach Autos mieten, allerdings sind die Mietpreise etwas teuer. Wenn man die Wüstenregionen, wie z.B. Wadi Rum erkunden will, ist ein gutes Allradfahrzeug unerläßlich.

Syrien Wie in Jordanien benötigt man einen Zollpassierschein, wenn man das eigene Auto oder Motorrad mitbringt. Zusätzlich braucht man die Fahrzeugzulassungspapiere und einen internationalen Führerschein. An der Grenze muß eine Haftpflichtversicherung zum Preis von US$36 pro Monat abgeschlossen werden. Der Wert dieser Versicherung ist fraglich und daher lohnt es sich, sicherzustellen, daß die eigene Versicherung in Syrien gültig ist – insbesondere, da einige Länder des Nahen Osten als "Kriegsgebiete" gelten. Lange Fahrten bei Nacht können gefährlich sein, da nicht alle Fahrer viel davon halten, die Scheinwerfer ständig anzuhaben.

Man kann Autos in Syrien mieten, allerdings kann die Auswahl ein bißchen begrenzt sein und es ist nicht billig. Es ist dennoch erwägenswert, besonders wenn man nicht alleine reist und vorhat, einige der schlecht erreichbaren Plätze zu besuchen.

Libanon Es gibt viele Autovermietungen im Libanon und die Preise sind konkurrenzfähig. Das Hauptproblem besteht in den gefährlichen Verkehrsbedingungen. Unfälle und Staus sind häufig, besonders in Beirut und auf der belebten Küstenstraße. Im Landes-inneren ist das Gelände bergig mit kurvigen, engen Straßen. Einige dieser Straßen werden im Winter geschlossen. Wenn man vorhat, den eigenen Wagen mitzunehmen, sollte man sich bei der Libanesischen Botschaft nach den Importzöllen erkundigen, da diese untragbar hoch sein können.

Fahrrad

Jordanien Fahrradfahren ist eine Möglichkeit in Jordanien aber nicht unbedingt eine spaßige. Die intensive Hitze im Sommer kann zu Hitzschlag und Dehydrierung führen, wenn man nicht vorsichtig ist. Gen Norden oder Süden (die Richtung der meisten Routen) wird das Fahrradfahren auch ziemlich anstrengend. Der starke Westwind kann zermürbend sein. Es empfiehlt sich, viele Ersatzteile mitzunehmen.

Syrien Nur wenige Leute fahren in Syrien Fahrrad, da das Klima, besonders im Sommer, nicht gerade dazu anregt. Die Hitze wie auch die Distanzen sind zu groß. Wie dem auch sei, wenn man unbedingt Radfahren will, gibt es keinen Hinderungsgrund - man sollte nur für genügend Ersatzteile sorgen, da diese vor Ort schwer erhältlich sind.

Libanon Die Verkehrsbedingungen machen Fahrradfahren auf den Hauptstraßen extrem gefährlich, wenn nicht geradezu selbstmörderisch. Die Gebirgsgebiete sind ideal zum Radfahren, wenn man ein Mountainbike hat. Doch man sei gewarnt: das Gelände ist extrem zerklüftet und man sollte sehr fit sein, um die Gebirgsstraßen anzugehen. Auch hier ist es eine gute Idee, viele Ersatzteile mitzuführen.

PETER JOUSIFFE

The remarkably well-preserved city of Jerash, Jordan

Cómo Movilizarse dentro de Jordania, Siria y Líbano

En Autobús

Jordania La manera más cómoda de viajar es en los enormes autobuses azules y blancos JEET que recorren las principales rutas turísticas de Jordania. Es importante encargar los pasajes con dos días de anticipación puesto que generalmente viajan llenos. Los autobuses privados, más pequeños, van practicamente a cualquier destinación que usted se pueda imaginar.

Las pequeñas poblaciones cuentan con un servicio de microbuses de 20 plazas que parten cuando se llenan. Los pasajes son baratos, pero puede que le cobren por todo el trayecto aunque usted no vaya hasta el final de la línea. Es una buena idea concretar el precio antes de emprender el viaje. A estos autobuses se les puede hacer señales para que se paren en cualquier punto de la ruta y, por lo general, si no van ya llenos, se pararán para que usted pueda subir.

Siria En Siria existen cuatro niveles de servicios de autobús, con los correspondientes cuatro niveles de tarifas. Los más caros y cómodos son los autobuses 'luxury' - entre los que están los operados por Qadmous, AL-Ahliah y Al-Ryan. Los pasajes deben comprarse con antelación (debido a la demanda) y estos autobuse operan según un horario - con puntualidad.

El servicio Karnak de autobuses operado por el gobierno, en el pasado se consideraba como el servicio de lujo de las carreteras de Siria, pero al presente, con tantas compañías rivales en operación con vehículos más rápidos y modernos, en comparación, Karnak se ha quedado rezagado. A pesar de lo dicho, estos autobuses están en perfectas condiciones y son algo más baratos que los autobuses de lujo. Antes de subir debe comprarse el pasaje, con asiento numerado. Los autobuses Karnak, por lo general, tienen estaciones en el centro de la ciudad, mientras que las estaciones de los autobuses de lujo, a veces, son algo más difíciles de localizar.

La compañía de autobuses Pullman ofrece un servicio similar. Pullman es una compañía semiprivada que opera según un horario fijo, pero muchas veces sus autobuses van muy llenos y viajan despacio. Los autobuses Pullman son un poco más baratos que los Karnak, pero no tan baratos como los típicos autobuses locales.

Los microbuses (conocidos localmente por *micros*) son furgonetas modernas modificadas para que puedan caber algunas personas más. Se utilizan principalmente para viajes cortos entre las ciudades y en muchas rutas a los pueblos pequeños y las villas. Por lo general, son caros y parten cuando se llenan. Debido a que son pequeños y no se permite viajar de pie, las salidas son mucho más frecuentes.

En el fondo de la escala del transporte encontramos los autobuses y los minibuses de edad difícil de determinar que habían sido el núcleo del sistema de transporte público por autobús en Siria hasta finales de la década de los 80. Estos autobuses son mucho menos cómodos que los modernos,

PETER AND ANN JOUSIFFE

Archaeological Museum artefact, Aleppo, Syria

pero si la distancia a recorrer no es larga la incomodidad no es problema serio y ofrecen una de las mejores oportunidades de mezclarse con la gente local. Los autobuses enlazan los pueblos más importantes y los minibuses operan en las distancias cortas y van a los lugares más aislados. Los minibuses tienen apariencia muy ordinaria desde fuera pero por dentro están decorados con una gran variedad de ornamentos llamativos. No siguen ningún horario y parten cuando están llenos. Generalmente, los viajes toman más tiempo que los de los otros autobuses puesto que los pasajeros se pueden apear o subir en cualquier punto de la ruta, de aquí el mote de *stop-stops* con que la gente local les ha bautizado. Los pasajes son baratos, aunque a veces, cobrarán un poco más en los minibuses que en los autobuses más grandes que cubren la misma ruta.

Precaución: Puede considerarse ofensivo que en el autobús un hombre se siente al lado de una mujer - por lo menos por las mujeres conservadoras de más edad. Si al subir un hombre solo encuentra un asiento libre al lado de una mujer local, lo más prudente es permanecer de pie. Frecuentemente, los pasajeros se cambian de asiento para que las mujeres puedan sentarse juntas o con los miembros de su familia y así dejar vacantes los asientos sobrantes. Si un hombre se sienta al lado de una mujer local y la gente empieza a agitarse, lo más prudente es no discutir.

Líbano La guerra civil dislocó el servicio público de autobuses pero, gradualmente, las cosas están mejorando. Ahora hay autobuses que circulan las rutas más importantes alrededor de Beirut, inclusive van al aeropuerto. Los precios de los pasajes son fijos y baratos y operan por el sistema de 'señal por dedo' También hay autobuses

que operan entre los pueblos más importantes del país, pero estos no tienen un horario fijo.

En Tren

Jordania En Jordania hay un tren semanal que conecta Amman con Damasco a lo largo de la vieja línea de ferrocarril de Hejaz. El resto de las líneas se usan exclusivamente para trenes de mercancías.

Siria Existe un servicio de pasajeros entre Damasco y Qamishle vía Aleppo, Deir-ez-Zor y Hassake. Tambieén hay trenes que operan en un par de vías secundarias. Una que va desde Aleppo a Lattakia y luego va por la costa a Tartus y sigue a Homs y Damasco. La línea ferroviaria que anteriormente iba de Damasco a Medina, en la Arabia Saudita, y llevaba a los peregrinos a La Meca, todavía tiene una parte en la que opera un tren lento dos veces por semana con máquina diesel (si a usted le gustan los trenes viejos, con un poco de suerte, puede que le toque viajar en uno arrastrado por una máquina de vapor) que va desde Damasco a Der'a. Una de estas líneas continúa hasta Hamman en Jordania. Durante el verano, los trenes siguen la ruta a lo largo del valle Barada.

En Siria los trenes son baratos y, a veces, puntuales, pero nunca hay más de tres servicios por día hacia cualquier destino en particular y muchas veces menos. Aún peor, las estaciones por lo general están ubicadas en sitios difíciles, a varios kilómetros del centro de la ciudad, así pues, a no ser que a usted le encanten mucho los trenes, le resultará más práctico tomar un autobús o un taxi. En los trenes, la primera clase está climatizada y tiene asientos parecidos a los de los aviones; la segunda clase es igual pero sin climatizar. También pueden obtenerse camas (mannama).

Líbano En el Líbano no han quedado servicios de pasajeros en operación y la mayoría de las viejas vías han sido desmanteladas, las han volado o han edificado encima, por lo tanto, no existen muchas probabilidades de que el servicio de ferrocarril sea restaurado. Hay planes para la construcción de una línea entre Beirut y Damasco.

Servicio de Taxis

Jordania El servicio de taxis opera en muchas rutas, los taxis parten cuando están llenos. Por lo general se llenan rápidamente ya que sólo tienen 5 ó 7 plazas. Cuestan el doble que los minibuses, pero son más rápidos y hacen menos paradas durante el viaje para recoger o dejar pasajeros.

Siria Este país tiene un sistema de 'taxis de servicio' (servis) que solamente opera a lo largo de las rutas más populares. Cuestan unas tres veces más que los autobuses pero tienen la ventaja de ir más rápidos y, debido a que sólo pueden llevar cinco pasajeros, se llenan más rápidamente.

Líbano Este país tiene un servicio conocido por 'taxis de servicio' (*servis*) además de los taxis ordinarios que pueden reconocerse por el color rojo de sus matrículas. Los taxis de servicio generalmente siguen una ruta predeterminada y usted puede indicarles que se paren diciendole al taxista 'indak' (aquí). Quizás tenga que tomar más de un taxi si su destino no está en una de las rutas presentes del taxista. Hasta hace poco, el servicio de taxis era la única forma de movilizarse y todavía continúan siendo una de las opciones favoritas. Los precios son baratos y pocas veces hay que esperar demasiado para poder indicar a uno que se pare.

PETER JOUSIFFE

Martyr's statue, Beirut, Lebanon

Los taxis ordinarios no están restringidos a seguir una ruta única y una vez alquilados no se paran para recoger a otros pasajeros. Pueden pedirse taxis por teléfono.

A veces, algunos coches que no son taxis autorizados, sino que pertenecen a personas que trabajan por su cuenta, se paran para ofrecer servicio. Si toma uno de estos coches asegúrese de acordar el precio del viaje de antemano.

Por Carretera

Jordania No tendrá problemas si quiere llevarse su propio vehículo a Jordania, pero necesitará un 'carnet de passage en douane' y seguro propio. La Asociación Automovilística del Reino Unido (the UK Automovile Association) pide una garantía en metálico para el carnet, que en realidad sirve para eliminar el importe de aduanas. Es muy importante que se rellene bien el carnet en cada frontera, de lo contrario puede que le pidan mucho dinero cuando salga del país.

Por lo general, la red de carreteras es buena y los conductores, comparados con otros en el medio oriente, no son demasiado erráticos. Se maneja por la derecha y la mayoría de los lugares a los que usted quiera dirigirse tendrán indicaciones en inglés y en árabe. En la carretera abierta el límite de velocidad es de 90 km/h y en la Autopista del Desierto 110 km/h.

En Jordania pueden alquilarse coches sin dificultad, pero las tarifas son bastante altas. Si quiere explorar las regiones desérticas como Wadi Rum, es esencial utilizar un vehículo de tracción a cuatro ruedas.

Siria Al igual que en Jordania, usted necesitará un 'carnet de passage en douane' si se lleva su coche o motocicleta. Además, necesitará los documentos de registración de su vehículo y una licencia internacional de conducir. El seguro contra terceras partes debe comprarse en la frontera y cuesta US$36,00 por mes. Existen dudas sobre el valor de este seguro y vale la pena que usted averigüe si su propio seguro le cubre en Siria, especialmente teniendo en cuenta que algunos países del medio oriente están considerados como 'zonas de guerra'. Los viajes nocturnos largos pueden ser peligrosos ya que no todos los conductores creen que es necesario usar los faros todo el tiempo.

Pueden alquilarse coches en Siria, pero la variedad es muy limitada y los precios son baratos. Pero debe considerarlo si va acompañado y tiene intención de visitar los lugares poco accesibles.

Líbano En Líbano existen muchas compañías de coches de alquiler y los precios son competitivos. El problema principal son las condiciones de tráfico peligrosas. Los accidentes y las congestiones de tráfico son frecuentes, particularmente en Beirut y en la ruta costeña. En el interior el terreno es montañoso y las carreteras son estrechas y con muchas curvas. Durante el invierno algunas de estas carreteras están cerradas. Si quiere tomar su propio vehículo es importante que chequee con la Embajada libanesa acerca de los impuestos de importación puesto que estos pueden ser extremadamente altos.

En Bicicleta

Jordania En Jordania puede considerarse la opción de movilizarse en bicicleta, pero esta no es una opción placentera. Si no va con cuidado, el intenso calor durante el verano puede producir insolación y deshidratación. Movilizarse hacia el norte o hacia el sur (la dirección princial de la mayoría de las rutas) puede ser trabajo duro. Hay vientos prevalentes del oeste que pueden fatigarle. Llévese muchos repuestos.

Siria Muy poca gente utiliza la bicicleta en Siria ya que el clima no se presta a ello, especialmente en verano. Las temperaturas son demasiado altas y las distancias demasiado largas. Por otra parte, si usted quiere movilizarse en bicicleta, nadie puede impedírselo, cerciórese de llevar repuestos ya que estos son difíciles de obtener.

Líbano Las condiciones del tráfico hacen la movilización en bicicleta extremadamente peligrosa, por no decir suicida. Las zonas montañosas son ideales para recorrerlas en bicicleta de montaña, pero le avisamos: el terreno es muy escabroso y tendrá que estar en buena forma para poder subir las rutas montañosas. Una vez más, es una buena idea llevar muchos recambios.

ヨルダン、シリア、レバノンの旅

バス

ヨルダン

ヨルダンを最も楽に旅するには、おもなツーリストコースを走っている青と白の巨大なジェット（JETT）バスが良い。満席になることがよくあるので忘れずに二日前に予約を入れること。これより小さい私営のバスは、ほとんどの地域を走っている。

小さい町には20席のミニバスが運行し、満員になり次第発車する。料金は安いが、途中下車しても全額払わなくてはいけない。乗車する前に料金を確認しよう。満員でなければ、路線上で合図をするとほとんどの場合車を止めてくれ、乗車できる。

シリア

シリアのバスは４つのクラスがありそれぞれ料金が異なる。最も高く乗り心地がいいのは「豪華」バスで、運営している会社にはカドモウス（Qadmous）、アル・アーリアー（Al-Ahliah）、アル・ライアン（Al-Ryan）がある。需要が大きいためチケットは前もって必ず予約すること。このタイプのバスは時刻表通りに出発する。

以前、国営のカルナック（Karnak）バスは、シリアの国道を走るバスの中では豪華なものとして知られていたが、現在は多くの競争会社がより速くスマートなバスを使うようになったため、これらと比較すると貧弱に見える。別の言い方をすれば、特に悪い所はないが、他の豪華バスよりは安いと

いうことだ。乗車する前に必ず指定席券を買うこと。カルナック・バスの発着場はふつう町の中心にあるが、豪華バスの会社は少し離れた所にあるので少々不便だ。

同様のサービスを行なうものにプルマン（Pullman）バス会社がある。プルマンは半私営で時刻表通りに運行するが、多少古くて遅い。これにも予約制度があるが、需要はあまり大きくない。プルマン・バスはカルナックよりわずかに安いが、古びたローカルバスほど安くはない。

マイクロバス（現地の言葉でミークロス－meecros－と呼ばれる）は近代的なバンで、何人か余分に詰め込めるように改造してある。市と市、小さい町や村を結ぶ数多くの短距離ルートを走る。一般的に料金は高めで、満員になると発車する。しかし、小さい上に立って乗車できないので、比較的頻繁に出発する。

道路輸送機関のうちランクが最も低いのはクラシックカーと見間違うほど古いバスとミニバスで、1980年代末までシリアの公共バス機関の大部分を占めていた。このバスは他の近代的な交通機関よりずっと乗り心地が悪いが、短距離なのでさほど気にならない。しかも、現地の人々と知り合うには最も良い方法だ。バスはすべての主要都市を結ぶが、ミニバスは様々な短距離路線を走り、遠隔地にも行く。ミニバスの外観は地味だが、内装は並外れて派手な装飾を施してある。

時刻表はなく、満員になりしだい発車する。行程の途中ならどこでも乗客を乗り降りさせるので、一般的に乗車時間は他のバスよりも長い。このため、現地の人にストップストップス（stop-stops）というニックネームで呼ばれている。料金は安いが、同じコースを走るバスよりもわずかに高いことがある。

注意：バスの車内で、女性のとなりに男性が座るのは失礼にあたるとされている。年配の保守的な女性にその傾向が強く見られる。現地女性の隣にしか席が空いていない場合、男性旅行客は立ったままでいるほうが賢明だ。乗客の側で、女性客同士、または家族同士が座れるようにアレンジし直し席をあけてくれることがしばしばある。男性の旅行客が現地の女性のとなりに座ったために他の乗客が反応を示すようだったら、逆らわないようにしたほうが良い。

レバノン

内戦により途絶え気味だったバスの運行が、最近次第に改善されてきた。空港を含むベイルート（Beirut）周辺の主要路線は全て運行している。低額の規定料金で、大声で呼び止めて乗るという方式だ。地方の主要な市町にもバスは運行しているが、時刻表はない。

電車

ヨルダン

ヨルダンでは毎週、旧ヘヤズ（Hejaz）鉄道沿いを運行す

るアンマン(Amman)ダマスカス(Damascus)を結ぶ電車が走っている。その他の線は上等の列車だけが使っている。

シリア

アレッポ(Aleppo)、デイル・エズ・ゾール(Deir ez-Zur)、ハサカ(Hassake)経由でダマスカスとカミシリイェ(Qamishle)を結ぶ乗客列車がある。また、列車は二級鉄道にも通っているが、そのひとつはアレッポからラタキア(Lattakia)、そして海岸線を通りタルトゥース(Tartus)まで行き、ホムス(Homs)とダマスカスまで通じている。ヘヤズ鉄道は、もともとメッカに信者を送るためにダマスカスからサウジアラビアのメディナ(Medina)までを走っていたが、その線の一部は今でもまだ使われている。週2回

遅いディーゼル車(たまに鉄道の好きな人が喜ぶ蒸気機関車)がダマスカスからデルアー(Der'a)まで走っている。このうちの1本はヨルダンのアンマンまで通る。夏期はバラダ(Barada)谷沿いを走る。

シリアの列車は料金が安くけっこう時間に正確だが、どの線も一日に3本を越えることはまずない。さらに、町の中心から2、3キロ離れた不便な所に駅があるので、鉄道愛好家でなければ、バスやタクシーのほうが便利でよい。一等車両はエアコン付きで飛行機タイプのシート、二等車両はエアコンがないことの他は一等と同じだ。寝台車(マナアマ：manaama)もある。

レバノン

レバノンでは乗客用の列車は未だに運行していない。

古いレールははぎとられたり、爆破されたり、建物でふさがれたりしているが、鉄道が敷かれる目処は立っていない。しかし、ベイルートからダマスカスまでの新鉄道の建設予定はある。

サービス・タクシー

ヨルダン

サービス・タクシーはたくさんの路線を運行していて、満員になり次第発車するシステム。5座席から7座席しかないので、ふつうはすぐに満員になる。料金はミニバスよりも最高2倍近いが、途中乗客の乗り降りが少ない分だけ速い。

シリア

この国のサービス・タクシー(サーヴィース：servees)は、最も人気がある道路沿いにしか走っていない。料金はバスより3倍近いが、速い

View to the necropolis, Palmyra (Tadmor), Syria

ということと乗客は5人までしか乗れないため、すぐに満員になるという利点がある。

レバノン

この国にはサービス・タクシー、そして赤いナンバープレートのタクシーがある。サービス・タクシーはふつう決まったルートを走っていて、「インダック(indak：ここという意)」と運転手に言えばどこでも止まってくれる。目的地が運転手の決まったルート上にない場合は、何回か他のサービス・タクシーに乗り換えなくてはいけないことがある。最近まで、サービス・タクシーは唯一の旅行手段だったが、現在でも人気がある。料金は安く、つかまえるのにほとんど待つ必要がない。

普通のタクシーはルートが決まっておらず、料金が一定だ。電話で予約できる。

しばしばフリーランスの車が止まるが、これは規定のタクシーではない。このような車に乗るときはあらかじめ料金を確認すること。

道路

ヨルダン

ヨルダンの自動車持ち込みは問題ないが、カルネ(自動車の無税許可証)と保険が必要だ。英国自動車協会(The UK Automobile Association)はカルネを作る時に保証金を要求するが、それは関税の権利破棄証書として有効だ。国境でカルネが正確に記入されているか必ず確認すること。そうでないと出国する際にお金をたくさん払わなくてはいけなくなることがある。

道路網は一般的によく発達していて、中近東の基準からすると、運転はさほどひどくない。自動車は右側通行で、道路標識は英語とアラビア語で表示されていることが多い。制限速度は見通しのいい道路で時速90キロ、砂漠高速道路(Desert Highway)で110キロだ。

レンタカーは比較的簡単にヨルダンで借りることができるが少し高い。ワジ・ルム(Wadi Rum)のような砂漠地帯を旅行する時はしっかりした四駆が必要だ。

シリア

自分の自動車やバイクを国内に持ち込む時はヨルダンと同じようにカルネが必要だ。それに加え、自動車登録証と国際免許も必要だ。国境で必ず1ヶ月US36ドルの第三者賠償責任保険に加入しなくてはならない。この保険は価値に疑問があるうえ、中近東諸国のいくつかは「戦争地帯」として考えられているので、上記の保険以外に自分自身が加入している保険がシリアをカバーしているか確認すること。ヘッドライトをつけない自動車もたまにあるので夜間の長距離運転は危険だ。

シリア国内でもレンタカーはあるが、種類が多少限られているうえ料金が高い。しかし、2人以上で遠隔地を旅する場合は交通手段の一つとして考えておいても良い。

レバノン

レバノンにはレンタカー会社がたくさんあり、値段も安い。一番の問題点は道路交通状態が危険だというこ

とだ。特に、ベイルートと交通量が多い海岸沿いの道では交通事故と渋滞がよく起こる。内陸部は山が険しく、道路はカーブが多くて狭い。このうちいくつかは冬期に通行止めになる。自分の自動車を持ち込む際には関税が大変高いのでレバノン大使館に問い合わせて確認すること。

自転車

ヨルダン

ヨルダンを自転車旅行するのは不可能ではないが、必ずしも楽しいとは言えない。夏は気を付けないと高温で日射病になったり脱水症状を起こしたりすることがある。北方向や南方向(ほとんどのルートは南北に走っている)をサイクリングするのも厳しい。西からは強い卓越風が吹くので疲労しやすい。部品を十分に持っていくこと。

シリア

気候、特に夏の暑さが厳しいため、シリアをサイクリングする旅行者はほとんどいない。大変暑く距離も長い。しかしどうしてもサイクリングをしたければ試してみると良い。ただし、現地で部品を入手することは難しいので十分に準備していくこと。

レバノン

主要道路のサイクリングは、道路の交通状態が悪いので自殺的と言っても良いほど大変危険だ。山岳地域はマウンテンバイクを持って行けば最高だが、この地域はとても険しいので山間部の道路を挑戦するには体力が必要。ここも十分に部品を持っていくように。

Index

Note: Geographical and cultural features are also listed separately at the end of the general index in their appropriate categories.

GENERAL INDEX

Al Abd (S) 19 H4
Al Abzam (S) 10 B6
Al Adasiyya (J) 44 C3
Al 'Adasiyya (J) 44 C6
Al Adliyeh (S) 39 F6
Al Ajamie (S) 44 D3
Al'al (J) 44 D3
Al 'Al (J) 48 C1
Al Alamein (S) 16 D5
Al Aluk (J) 44 D5
Al A'lyaneh (S) 40 D3
Al Amiriyeh (S) 13 E4
Al Amiriyya (J) 48 D2
Alamiyah (S) 11 E5
Al Amoudiyeh (S) 17 G6
Al Annazeh (S) 16 B4
Alan'nazeh (S) 16 B5
Al Anqawie (S) 16 C2
Al 'Anz (S) 17 H1
Al A'riemeh (S) 11 E4
Al Ariesheh (S) 13 E4
Al Aritayn (J) 45 G6
Al Asadiyeh (S) 13 E3
Al Asadiyeh (S) 13 F2
Al Asadiyeh (S) 16 D1
Ala'seebeh (S) 16 E4
Al Ashra (S) 13 F4
Al Ashrafiyeh (S) 16 D6
Al Ashrafiyya (J) 44 C4
Al Aslaha (S) 45 E3
Al Atneh (S) 39 G4
Al Atshaneh (S) 14 B2
Al Auja (J) 53 F4
Al 'Ayn Al Bayda (J) 48 B5
Al Azraq Al Janubi (J) 49 G1
Al Bab (S) 10 D5
Al Bade'e (S) 12 A4
Al Bahlouliyeh (S) 16 B2
Al Bahra (S) 20 B6
Al Baidah (S) 13 F4
Al Ba'il (J) 45 E4
Ali Bajliyeh (S) 12 A4
Albalouta (S) 16 A1
Al Baq'a (J) 44 C6
Al Baqura (J) 44 C3
Al-Bara (Al-Kafr) (S) 16 C2
Al Barakheh (S) 16 C2
Al Baridah (S) 40 B2
Al Barkeh (S) 39 F6
Al Bas'ah (S) 19 F2
Albashiyeh (S) 13 H4
Al Basira (S) 20 A4
Al Basiri (S) 40 B3
Albas'sa (S) 16 A3
Al Batma (S) 17 E6
Al Bayda Al Gharbiyeh (S) 39 H2
Al Bayniyeh (S) 11 F4
Al Bayyadiyeh (S) 16 C5
Al Baziyeh (S) 10 B4
Al Beitariyeh (S) 39 F6
Al Biezeh (S) 11 E5
Al Bishriyya (S) 45 F5
Al Biyeh (S) 16 D5
Al Bizara (S) 13 G4
Al Breij (S) 39 G2
Al Budi (S) 16 B3
Albu'isa (S) 19 F2
Al Burbayta (J) 48 C4
Al Busayt (SA) 54 C2
Al Buweid (S) 17 E3
Al Bweider (S) 17 F2
Al Bweir (S) 17 E6
Al Dweira (S) 45 E2
Aleppo (Halab) (S) 10 C6
Aley (L) 31 F1
Al Fadghamie (S) 20 B1
Al Faj (S) 13 H5
Alfajir (S) 16 A2

Al Fakhoura (S) 16 B3
Al Faqie'e (S) 44 D2
Al Fayha' (J) 48 C1
Al Fedah (S) 45 G3
Al Foua'a (S) 10 A6
Al Fruqlos (S) 17 E6
Al Fsaqin (L) 31 E2
Al Fuhays (J) 44 C6
Al Fundo (S) 10 A6
Al Furat River (Ir) 43 F2
Al Fursan (S) 11 E3
Al Gammashiyeh (S) 16 C3
Al Ghalyo (S) 12 B4
Al Ghandura (S) 11 E4
Alghanto (S) 16 D5
Al Gharat (S) 11 E4
Alghariyeh (S) 45 F4
Alghas'saniyeh (S) 16 A1
Al Ghassaniyeh (S) 16 C1
Al Ghazli (S) 12 B5
Al Ghazzawiyeh (S) 10 B5
Al Ghizlanigh (S) 39 F6
Alghor (S) 10 D4
Alghrraf (S) 10 A6
Al Ghuz (S) 17 E4
Al Habbab (S) 11 G3
Al Habbariyeh (S) 37 H5
Al Habeit (S) 16 C3
Al Hader (S) 17 E4
Al Haditha (SA) 49 H3
Al Haffeh (S) 16 B2
Al Hafneh (S) 18 B6
Al Hafr (S) 39 G2
Alhajar (S) 16 B2
Al Hajeb (S) 17 F1
Al Hakimeh (S) 17 F1
Al Halbeh (S) 41 E3
Al Haleh (S) 19 E1
Al Hameh (S) 33 E5
Al Hamidayah (S) 16 A6
Al Hammam (S) 18 C1
Al'hamoud (S) 11 F6
Al Hamra (J) 44 D4
Al Hamra (S) 17 E4
Al Hamraat (S) 39 G1
Al Hamtlaniyah (S) 17 E3
Alhaqaf (S) 45 F2
Al Harieseh (S) 45 G4
Al Harra (S) 37 G6
Al Hasa (J) 48 D5
Al Hasaneh (S) 12 B4
Al Hashimiyya (J) 44 D5
Al Hashimiyya (J) 48 C6
Al Hasrat (S) 20 B6
Al Hattan (S) 16 C3
Al Hawa (S) 13 F4
Al Hawash (S) 16 C3
Al Hawayer (S) 17 E4
Al Hawi (S) 19 F2
Al Hawiyeh (S) 45 G4
Alheimar (S) 11 F3
Al Heisheho (S) 16 A6
Al Hesheh (S) 12 A5
Al Hijjeh (S) 44 D2
Alhilwaniyeh (S) 11 F3
Al Himma (J) 44 C4
Al Hmeimeh (S) 16 D6
Al Hmera (S) 11 E4
Al Hmera (S) 12 B4
Al Hmera (S) 39 G3
Al Hmeri (S) 16 C5
Al Hol (S) 13 H5
Al Hosh (S) 32 C4
Alhour (S) 16 B2
Al Hoz (S) 24 C2
Al Hrak (S) 45 E3
Al Hraki (S) 17 E6

Al Hsain (S) 20 B2
Al Hseniyeh (S) 37 H3
Al Hulou (S) 13 E3
Al Humayma Al Jadida (J) 52 B3
Al Huriyeh (S) 11 H3
Al Huriyyeh (S) 11 G6
Al Hurriyeh (S) 20 B3
Al Husainiyeh (S) 16 C1
Al Husaynuyya (J) 48 C1
Al Huseiniya (J) 48 C4
Al Hweijeh (S) 11 G5
Al Hweijeh (S) 13 G4
Al Hweijeh (S) 16 C3
Al Isawiyah (SA) 50 C6
Al Izzeh (S) 13 F5
Al Jafr (J) 53 E2
Aljalouniyeh (S) 16 C1
Aljanat (S) 20 B2
Al Jarniyeh (S) 33 G2
Al Kabar (S) 19 G2
Alkabeer (S) 16 B1
Al Kabireh (S) 19 E2
Alkaf (S) 39 G2
Al Kafr (S) 45 F3
Al Kaltah (S) 12 A6
Al Kamsha (S) 44 C5
Al Kanayes (S) 16 D2
Al Karak (S) 45 E3
Al Karameh (S) 19 E1
Al Karimeh (S) 16 B6
Al Kashkiyeh (S) 20 B6
Al Kashmeh (S) 20 C6
Al Kawn Al Ahmar (J) 45 E4
Al Kazimiyeh (S) 14 D1
Al Khadra (S) 10 B4
Al Khafseh (S) 11 F5
Al Khaldiyeh (S) 17 F6
Al Khaldiyeh (S) 45 F2
Al Khalfitli (S) 10 D4
Al Khalidiyya (J) 45 E5
Al Khalta (S) 12 B5
Al Kharabeh (S) 16 B6
Al Kharayej (S) 20 B6
Al Kharijeh (S) 17 F5
Al Kharita (S) 13 F4
Al Khatib (S) 16 C3
Al Khazneh (S) 45 G4
Al Khirba As Samra (J) 44 D5
Al Khmesiyeh (S) 19 F2
Al Kisrah (S) 19 G2
Al Kisweh (S) 39 E6
Al Koiah (J) 44 C3
Al Kom (S) 18 C4
Al Kseib (S) 45 F3
Al Kufayr (J) 44 D5
Al Lajjun (J) 48 C3
Al Laqbeh (S) 16 C4
Allij (S) 16 C2
Alma (S) 45 E3
Al Ma'adamiyeh (S) 33 E6
Al Maboujeh (S) 17 F4
Al Madabe'e (S) 17 E6
Al M'adammiyeh (S) 39 G4
Al Madaniyeh (S) 13 G6
Al Mafar (S) 13 H5
Al Maghara (S) 11 F4
Al Mahatta (S) 45 E2
Al Mahatta Ath'thania (S) 42 C2
Al Mahdoom (S) 11 E6
Al Majdal (J) 44 C5
Al Majdal (S) 16 D4
Al Majwa (S) 16 C5
Al-Malkyer (S) 14 D1
Al Ma'mura (S) 33 G2
Al Manajier (S) 13 E4
Al Manakhir (J) 44 D6
Al Manara (S) 12 B4

Al Manasif (S) 20 B4
Almanathira (S) 16 A1
Al Ma'neyh (S) 24 C3
Al Mankhar (S) 12 B6
Al Manshiyya (J) 44 C3
Al Manshiyya (J) 52 C1
Al-Mansura (S) 18 C1
Al Mashamies (S) 17 E2
Al-Mashari'a (J) 44 B4
Al Mashbak (S) 10 B5
Al Mashiyeh (S) 39 E6
Almashrafeh (S) 16 B6
Al Masiadeh (S) 14 C2
Al Maslakha (S) 20 B6
Al Maslakha (S) 20 B6
Al Mas'oudiyeh (S) 12 A5
Al Masrab (S) 19 G3
Al Mastumeh (S) 16 D1
Al Masudeh (S) 17 F5
Al Matab (S) 19 F2
Al Mataiyeh (S) 45 E4
Al Matalleh (S) 39 F6
Al Matalleh (S) 45 E2
Al Mazar As Shamali (J) 44 C4
Al Mazbal (S) 17 F5
Al Maziuneh (S) 11 G6
Al Mazra'a (S) 13 G4
Al Mazra'a (S) 13 H5
Al Mazra'a (S) 45 F3
Al Meedan (S) 17 E6
Al M'ez (S) 13 H5
Al Mghayer (S) 45 F4
Al Miffridat (J) 45 E5
Al Mina (L) 22 C4
Al Mis'awieeh (S) 13 F4
Al Mishirfeh (S) 17 G2
Al Mishrfeh (Fletah) (S) 29 F4
Al Mismiyeh (S) 45 E1
Al Mistafawiyeh (S) 14 C2
Al Mjeifer (S) 45 F3
Al Mleiha (S) 33 G6
Al Mnezra (S) 45 F4
Al Mou'ah (S) 16 D5
Al Mozarah (S) 16 C2
Al Mrah (S) 39 G4
Almreijeh (S) 16 B5
Al Mrejeb (S) 17 E3
Al Msfifra (S) 45 E3
Almsheirfeh (S) 16 B3
Al Msherfeh (S) 12 B5
Al Mthamneh (S) 10 D4
Al Mtouneh (S) 45 F2
Al Mughayyir (J) 44 D3
Al Mukhayba Al Tahta (J) 44 C3
Al Muraygha (S) 52 C3
Al Mushanaf (S) 45 F3
Al Mushtarakeh (S) 19 F2
Almustaba (J) 44 C5
Al Mutawssta (S) 17 E2
Al Muwaqqar (J) 48 D1
Al Mzeir'aa (S) 16 B3
Al Mzeneh (S) 16 C6
Al Nairab (S) 16 D1
Al Qaboun (S) 33 F5
Al-Qaddisiyyeh (J) 48 B6
Al Qadi (S) 11 E3
Al Qadmus (S) 16 B4
Al Qahtaniyeh (S) 14 B2
Al Qahtaniyeh (S) 14 C2
Al Qa'im (Ir) 43 F2
Al Qamsiyeh (S) 16 B5
Al Qanat (Ir) 14 D3
Al Qanjara (S) 16 A2
Al Qaryatein (S) 40 A2
Alqasbiyeh (S) 16 D6
Al Qasr (S) 10 B6
Al Qastal (J) 48 D1
Al Qastal (S) 10 B3

Wadi al Mu'ayzil (S) 40 D2
Wadi Al Muhaysh (J) 52 D5
Wadi al Muhazzam (S) 41 F1
Wadi al Mulusi (Ir) 42 B6
Wadi Al Murda (J) 47 F3
Wadi Al Mushaiyysh (J) 48 D5
Wadi al Rawdah (S) 40 B2
Wadi Al Wala (J) 48 C2
Wadi al Wa'r (S) 42 C2
Wadi Al-Yabes (J) 44 B4
Wadi Araba (J) 48 A6
Wadi Araba (J) 52 A4
Wadi ar Radd (S) 14 A4
Wadi ar Ratgah (Ir) 43 E2
Wadi ash Sha'lan (S) 41 F6
Wadi Ash Shidiyya (J) 52 D3
Wadi as Sawab (Ir) 42 A5
Wadi as Sawt (S) 40 D4
Wadi as-Seer (J) 44 C6
Wadi As Sibhi (J) 50 A1
Wadi Bayir (J) 49 H5
Wadi Dubavah (S) 18 D5
Wadi El Dabi (J) 49 F2
Wadi El Ghadaf (J) 49 F3
Wadi el Gharz (S) 45 H2
Wadi El Hassan (J) 49 H6
Wadiel'iyoun (S) 16 B5
Wadi el Kerak (J) 48 B3
Wadi el Mabrak (SA) 52 A6
Wadi El Makhruq (J) 49 G4
Wadi esh Safawi abu Qudar (J)
    45 G5
Wadi Hadraj (SA) 54 D1
Wadi Hafir (J) 52 A4
Wadi Hawran (Ir) 43 G5
Wadi Heidan (J) 48 C2
Wadi Hudruj (J) 54 A2
Wadi Husuydat Al Ghusaiya (J)
    49 H4
Wadi Husuydat Umm Nakhla (J)
    49 H4
Wadi ibn Hammad (J) 48 B3
Wadi Jarrah (S) 14 B3
Wadi Jilad (J) 45 G5
Wadi Madrasah (S) 16 D2
Wadi Maghar (J) 49 E5
Wadi Mudeisisat (J) 49 F1
Wadi Mujib (J) 48 C2
Wadi Musa (J) 52 C1
Wadi Musa (J) 52 C2
Wadi Mushash Al Kabid (J) 53 E4
Wadi Rajil (J) 49 G1
Wadir'rameen (S) 16 B2
Wadi Rum (J) 52 B5
Wadi Rumaylah (S) 14 B3
Wadi Rutaymi (S) 42 C3
Wadi Ruwayita (J) 53 E5
Wadi Ruweishid El Qisb (J) 47 E5
Wadi Sabil (J) 52 B5
Wadi Sahb Al Abyad (J) 54 A3
Wadi Shatnat al Milyaha (S) 18 A2
Wadi Shatnat Nabaj (S) 18 B2
Wadi Shatnat Saharij (S) 18 C2
Wadi Shu'ayb (J) 44 C6
Wadi Sirhan (SA) 50 B5
Wadi Suh Murrah (S) 40 C5
Wadi 'Ukash (Ir) 42 D3
Wadi Ukhaidir (J) 49 G5
Wadi Umm el Jurtayn (SA) 52 A6
Wadi Umm Haraq (J) 52 C5
Wadi Umm Tuways (J) 46 D6
Wadi Zarqa (J) 48 B2
Wahat Al Azraq (J) 49 G1
Wajhil'bahr (S) 16 C6
Wakalet Sana (S) 39 G6
Walgha (S) 45 F3
Walid'dabaghien (S) 17 F3
Waqm (S) 45 E2

Waqqas (J) 44 C4
Wardia (Ir) 14 B5
Warideh (S) 17 E6
Watal'khan (S) 16 B2
Waza'iyeh (S) 17 E6

Yabroud (S) 29 G5
Yafa (Is) 44 A3
Ya'four (S) 32 D5
Yağmuralan (T) 12 C2
Yahchouch (L) 26 D3
Yahmour (S) 10 C4
Yajuz (J) 44 C6
Yalankoz (T) 10 A4
Yalanli (S) 11 E4
Yammouné (L) 27 H3
Yanar (L) 31 E2
Yannouh (L) 35 H3
Yanoub (L) 27 F3
Yanta (L) 32 B4
Yaqusah (S) 44 C3
Yardımcı (T) 12 A2
Yarine (L) 35 G5
Yarmouk University (J) 44 D4
Yaroun (L) 36 A6
Yarqa (J) 44 C6
Yarzé (L) 26 B6
Yater (L) 35 H5
Yavuzlu (T) 10 C3
Yayladağı (T) 16 B1
Yayvantepe (T) 14 B1
Yeditepe (T) 16 B1
Yemişli (T) 14 A1
Yenisehir (T) 10 A5
Yohmor (L) 31 G6
Yohmor (L) 36 B3
Yolağzı (T) 11 E3
Yolbaşı (T) 10 B3
Yotvata Hai Bar Reserve (Is) 52 A3
Younine (L) 28 B3
Yukarı Beylerbeyi (T) 10 D2

Zaaitra (L) 26 D3
Zaarouriyé (L) 31 E4
Za'azuah (S) 12 B4
Zabadani (S) 32 D3
Zabarie (S) 19 H4
Zabboud (J) 28 C1
Zabbougha (L) 26 D5
Zabdeen (S) 33 G6
Zabqine (L) 35 G5
Zaghbar (S) 39 F6
Zaghibeh (S) 17 E3
Zahabiyeh (S) 16 C6
Zahed (S) 16 B6
Zahiyeh (S) 10 C4
Zahlé (L) 27 F6
Zahr'arab (S) 13 F2
Zai National Park (J) 44 C5
Zakier (S) 45 F2
Zakyeh (S) 39 E6
Zalabiyyeh (S) 19 G2
Zalga (L) 26 C6
Zama (S) 16 B3
Zamalka (S) 33 G5
Zammar (S) 17 E1
Zamrin (S) 16 A5
Zanbaq (S) 12 A4
Zane (L) 27 E1
Zaoutar ech Charqiyé (L) 36 B2
Zaoutar el Gharbiyé (L) 36 B2
Zarah (S) 16 C6
Zardana (S) 10 B6
Zarkonak (S) 11 F3
Zarqa (J) 44 D6
Zarzarita (S) 10 B5
Zayadiyeh (S) 10 D4
Zbeira (S) 45 E2

Zebdine (L) 36 B2
Zedal (S) 16 D6
Zeeban (S) 20 B5
Zefta (L) 30 D6
Zeinab (S) 33 F6
Zeitan (S) 10 C6
Zetan (S) 10 C5
Zgharta (L) 22 D4
Zgher Shamiyeh (S) 19 G3
Zhalta (L) 31 E5
Zieban (S) 20 A5
Zi'ebaqiyeh (S) 12 B4
Zighrine (L) 23 H4
Zighrine et Tahta (L) 24 A4
Ziyara (S) 10 D4
Zlaqiyat (S) 16 D4
Zoar (J) 48 B4
Zoghar (S) 11 E3
Zouaitini (J) 23 H5
Zouarib (L) 23 F3
Zouheir Al Kurdiyeh (S) 14 D1
Zouq el Mqachrine (L) 23 E3
Zouq Hadara (L) 23 E3
Zouq Mkave (L) 26 C5
Zouq Mosbeh (L) 26 C5
Zrariyé (L) 35 H2
Zrazir (L) 28 A2
Zughrien (S) 16 A2
Zughrien (S) 17 E4
Zulof (S) 11 E4
Zumrien (S) 37 H6

CAPES & HEADLANDS

Ras Abarouh (L) 30 C5
Ras Ach Chekka (L) 22 A5
Ras Beyrouth (L) 26 A6
Ras ech Chaq (L) 30 B6
Ras ed Dreijat (L) 35 F5
Ras el Baghlat (L) 35 E5
Ras el Biyada (L) 35 F4
Ras el Miassi (L) 35 E5
Ras el Mousri (L) 30 D2
Ras en Nabi Younés (L) 30 C3
Ras en Naqoura (Is) 35 E5
Ras es Sadiyat (L) 30 D3
Ras et Tair (L) 26 C4
Ras Ibn Hani (S) 16 A2
Ras Minet Bou Zeid (L) 35 G2
Ras Minet Chourane (L) 35 G2
Ras Minet er Rass (L) 35 F3
Ras Nabaa Mheilib (L) 35 G2
Ras Saharé (L) 30 C4
Ras Siddine el Bahr (L) 35 G2

ISLANDS

Arwad Island (S) 16 A5
Baqar Island (L) 22 C4
Bella Island (L) 22 C3
Laoukas Island (L) 22 C3
Mdoura Island (L) 22 C3
Palmier Island (L) 22 C3
Ramkine Island (L) 22 B3
Sanâni Island (L) 22 C3
Taouîlé Island (L) 22 C3
Toûroûs Island (L) 22 C3

MOUNTAINS & VALLEYS

Aarid el Haoua (L) 27 G5
Aarid el Kebir (L) 31 G5
Ad Daww (S) 40 B2
Ajjibal Attadmur Iyeh
    Aljanoubiyeh (S) 40 A3-C2
Ajjibal Attadmur Iyeh Ash
    Shamaliyeh (S) 18 B5
Ajlun Hills (J) 44 C4
Al Auja (J) 53 F4
Al Busayt (SA) 54 C2
Al Ghab (S) 16 C2

Al Manasif (S) 20 B4
Anti Lebanon (Jabal Lubnan Al-
    Sharqi) (L) 28 C6
Ard as Suwwam (J) 49 G6
Ard el Aali (L) 23 G2
Ard el Kichek (L) 28 D4
Ard el Kroum (L) 24 B4
Ard el Mouled (L) 22 D5
Ard el Qamar (L) 24 C4
Ard er Ras (L) 24 A6
Ard es Skaf (L) 24 B4
Arz Tannourine (L) 27 G1
Ash Shamah (SA) 50 B2
As Safa (S) 45 H1
Bekaa Valley (L) 28 B3, 32 B2
Chaltoun (L) 27 E1
Charbiné (L) 23 H4
Chebreqiyé (L) 32 A2
Chmis el Maaisra (L) 28 D2
Chmiss Ouakr ed Dabaa (L) 32 A4
Chouf Mountains (L) 31 F3
Dahr ech Chir (L) 31 H1
Dahr ech Choumar (L) 22 C6
Dahr el Arz (L) 27 F1
Dahr el Bouaider (L) 27 G3
Dahr el Haoua (L) 29 E3
Dahr el Mghar (L) 35 G1
Dahr el Moghr (L) 27 F6
Dahr el Qadib (L) 27 G3
Dahr el Qassissiyé (L) 27 F6
Dahr es Souss (L) 27 F1
Dhour Ain ej Jaouz (L) 37 E2
Dhour el Khanzir (L) 29 F2
Dibek Dağı (T) 14 B1
Ed Darjé (L) 31 G5
El Arz (L) 27 E2
El Baazoun (L) 22 D5
El Ghor (J) 48 B4
El Lisan (J) 48 B3
El Mafassekh (L) 31 F4
El Marj (L) 36 C3
El Mastabé (L) 27 H2
Er Rouss (L) 32 C2
Es Sedr (L) 27 H5
Fam el Mizab (L) 23 E6
Faydat (S) 19 E6
Gebel An-Nusariyah (S) 16 B3
Gebel Oustani (S) 16 C1
Gibal Hudruj (SA) 54 C2
Halimet Qarah (S) 29 F2
Harf Sannine (L) 27 F5
Horch Beit Habchi (L) 27 H2
Horch Beit Matta (L) 27 H2
Horch Enden (L) 23 E6
Hula Valley (Is) 36 C5
Jaafar (L) 23 H4
Jabal Aabrine (L) 22 B6
Jabal Aamar (L) 23 E5
Jabal Aamel (L) 35 H4
Jabal Aarbi (L) 31 G5
Jabal Aitou (L) 22 D6
Jabal Akroum (L) 23 H3
Jabal al Abyad (S) 17 H6
Jabal al Bishri (S) 19 E4
Jabal al Ghurab (S) 41 G3
Jabal Al Harad (J) 52 D4
Jabal al Hass (S) 17 F1
Jabal Al Khash (J) 52 C6
Jabal al Marah (S) 17 F1
Jabal Al Qannasiyah (J) 52 C4
Jabal An Nasla (J) 50 B2
Jabal an Niqniqiyeh (S) 40 C2
Jabal Antar (S) 32 D6
Jabal as Safra' (S) 18 B6
Jabal as Satih (S) 18 C6
Jabal at Tanf (S) 41 F5
Jabal At Tubayq (SA) 53 H5

LONELY PLANET GUIDES TO THE MIDDLE EAST

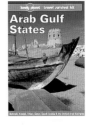

Arab Gulf States
This comprehensive, practical guide to travel in the Arab Gulf States covers travel in Bahrain, Kuwait, Oman, Qatar, Saudi Arabia and the United Arab Emirates. A concise history and language section is included for each country.

Iran
As well as practical travel details, the author provides background information that will fascinate adventurers and armchair travellers alike.

Israel & the Palestinian Territories
Float on the Dead Sea; go camel trekking in the Negev; volunteer for a unique kibbutz experience; and explore the holy city of Jerusalem and cosmopolitan Tel Aviv. This guide is packed with insight and practical information for all budgets.

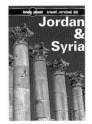

Jordan & Syria
Two countries with a wealth of natural and historical attractions for the adventurous travellers...12th-century Crusader castles, ruined cities and haunting desert landscapes.

Middle East on a shoestring
All the travel advice and essential information for travel in Afghanistan, Bahrain, Egypt, Iran, Iraq, Israel, Jordan, Kuwait, Lebanon, Oman, Qatar, Saudi Arabia, Syria, Turkey, United Arab Emirates and Yemen.

Trekking in Turkey
Explore beyond Turkey's coastline and you will be surprised to discover that Turkey has mountains to rival those found in Nepal.

Turkey
Experience Turkey with this highly acclaimed, best-selling guide. Packed with information for the traveller on any budget, it's your essential companion.

Turkish phrasebook
Practical words and phrases and a handy pronunciation guide make this phrasebook essential for travellers visiting Turkey.

Yemen
Discover the timeless history and intrigue of the land of the *Arabian Nights* with the most comprehensive guide to Yemen.

Also available:

The Gates of Damascus by Lieve Joris (translated by Sam Garrett)
This best-selling book is a beautifully drawn portrait of day-to-day life in modern Syria. Through her intimate contact with local people, Lieve Joris draws us into the fascinating world that lies behind the gates of Damascus.

LONELY PLANET PRODUCTS

AFRICA
Africa on a shoestring • Arabic (Moroccan) phrasebook • Cape Town city guide • Central Africa • East Africa • Egypt • Egypt travel atlas • Ethiopian (Amharic) phrasebook • Kenya • Morocco • North Africa • South Africa, Lesotho & Swaziland • Swahili phrasebook • Trekking in East Africa• West Africa • Zimbabwe, Botswana & Namibia • Zimbabwe, Botswana & Namibia travel atlas

ANTARCTICA
Antarctica

AUSTRALIA & THE PACIFIC
Australia • Australian phrasebook • Bushwalking in Australia • Bushwalking in Papua New Guinea • Fiji • Fijian phrasebook • Islands of Australia's Great Barrier Reef • Melbourne city guide • Micronesia • New Caledonia • New South Wales & the ACT • New Zealand • Northern Territory • Outback Australia • Papua New Guinea • Papua New Guinea phrasebook • Queensland • Rarotonga & the Cook Islands • Samoa • Solomon Islands • South Australia • Sydney city guide • Tahiti & French Polynesia • Tasmania • Tonga • Tramping in New Zealand • Vanuatu • Victoria • Western Australia
Travel Literature: Islands in the Clouds • Sean & David's Long Drive

CENTRAL AMERICA & THE CARIBBEAN
Central America on a shoestring • Costa Rica • Cuba • Eastern Caribbean • Guatemala, Belize & Yucatán: La Ruta Maya • Jamaica

EUROPE
Austria • Baltic States & Kaliningrad • Baltics States phrasebook • Britain • Central Europe on a shoestring • Central Europe phrasebook • Czech & Slovak Republics • Denmark • Dublin city guide • Eastern Europe on a shoestring • Eastern Europe phrasebook • Finland • France • Greece • Greek phrasebook • Hungary • Iceland, Greenland & the Faroe Islands • Ireland • Italy • Mediterranean Europe on a shoestring • Mediterranean Europe phrasebook • Paris city guide • Poland • Prague city guide • Russia, Ukraine & Belarus • Russian phrasebook • Scandinavian & Baltic Europe on a shoestring • Scandinavian Europe phrasebook • Slovenia • St Petersburg city guide • Switzerland • Trekking in Greece • Trekking in Spain • Ukrainian phrasebook • Vienna city guide • Walking in Switzerland • Western Europe on a shoestring • Western Europe phrasebook

INDIAN SUBCONTINENT
Bangladesh • Bengali phrasebook • Delhi city guide • Hindi/Urdu phrasebook • India • India & Bangladesh travel atlas • Indian Himalaya • Karakoram Highway • Nepal • Nepali phrasebook • Pakistan • Sri Lanka • Sri Lanka phrasebook • Trekking in the Indian Himalaya • Trekking in the Nepal Himalaya
Travel Literature: Shopping for Buddhas

ISLANDS OF THE INDIAN OCEAN
Madagascar & Comoros • Maldives & Islands of the East Indian Ocean • Mauritius, Réunion & Seychelles

MIDDLE EAST & CENTRAL ASIA
Arab Gulf States • Arabic (Egyptian) phrasebook • Central Asia • Iran • Israel & the Palestinian Territories • Israel & the Palestinian Territories travel atlas • Jordan & Syria • Jordan, Syria & Lebanon travel atlas • Middle East • Turkey • Turkish phrasebook • Trekking in Turkey • Yemen
Travel Literature: The Gates of Damascus

NORTH AMERICA
Alaska • Backpacking in Alaska • Baja California • California & Nevada • Canada • Hawaii • Honolulu city guide • Los Angeles city guide • Mexico • Miami city guide • New England • New Orleans city guide • Pacific Northwest USA • Rocky Mountain States • San Francisco city guide • Southwest USA • USA phrasebook

NORTH-EAST ASIA
Beijing city guide • Cantonese phrasebook • China • Hong Kong city guide • Hong Kong, Macau & Canton • Japan • Japanese phrasebook • Japanese audio pack • Korea • Korean phrasebook • Mandarin phrasebook • Mongolia • Mongolian phrasebook • North-East Asia on a shoestring • Seoul city guide • Taiwan • Tibet • Tibet phrasebook • Tokyo city guide
Travel Literature: Lost Japan

SOUTH AMERICA
Argentina, Uruguay & Paraguay • Bolivia • Brazil • Brazilian phrasebook • Buenos Aires city guide • Chile & Easter Island • Chile & Easter Island travel atlas • Colombia • Ecuador & the Galápagos Islands • Latin American Spanish phrasebook • Peru • Quechua phrasebook • Rio de Janeiro city guide • South America on a shoestring • Trekking in the Patagonian Andes • Venezuela
Travel Literature: Full Circle: A South American Journey

SOUTH-EAST ASIA
Bali & Lombok • Bangkok city guide • Burmese phrasebook• Cambodia • Ho Chi Minh city guide • Indonesia • Indonesian phrasebook • Indonesian audio pack • Jakarta city guide • Java • Laos • Laos travel atlas • Lao phrasebook • Malaysia, Singapore & Brunei • Myanmar (Burma) • Philippines • Pilipino phrasebook • Singapore city guide • South-East Asia on a shoestring • Thailand • Thailand travel atlas • Thai phrasebook • Thai Hill Tribes phrasebook • Thai audio pack • Vietnam • Vietnamese phrasebook • Vietnam travel atlas

PLANET TALK

Lonely Planet's FREE quarterly newsletter

We love hearing from you and think you'd like to hear from us.

When...is the right time to see reindeer in Finland?
Where...can you hear the best palm-wine music in Ghana?
How...do you get from Asunción to Areguá by steam train?
What...is the best way to see India?

For the answer to these and many other questions read PLANET TALK.

Every issue is packed with up-to-date travel news and advice including:

- a letter from Lonely Planet co-founders Tony and Maureen Wheeler
- go behind the scenes on the road with a Lonely Planet author
- feature article on an important and topical travel issue
- a selection of recent letters from travellers
- details on forthcoming Lonely Planet promotions
- complete list of Lonely Planet products

To join our mailing list contact any Lonely Planet office.

Also available: Lonely Planet T-shirts. 100% heavyweight cotton.

LONELY PLANET ONLINE

Get the latest travel information before you leave or while you're on the road

Whether you've just begun planning your next trip, or you're chasing down specific info on currency regulations or visa requirements, check out the Lonely Planet World Wide Web site for up-to-the-minute travel information.

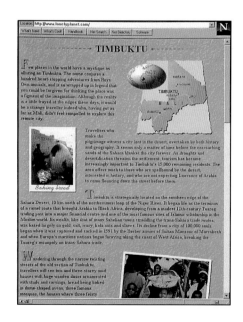

As well as travel profiles of your favourite destinations (including interactive maps and full-colour photos), you'll find current reports from our army of researchers and other travellers, updates on health and visas, travel advisories, and the ecological and political issues you need to be aware of as you travel.

There's an online travellers' forum (the Thorn Tree) where you can share your experiences of life on the road, meet travel companions and ask other travellers for their recommendations and advice. We also have plenty of links to other Web sites useful to independent travellers.

With tens of thousands of visitors a month, the Lonely Planet Web site is one of the most popular on the Internet and has won a number of awards including GNN's Best of the Net travel award.

http://www.lonelyplanet.com

LONELY PLANET TRAVEL ATLASES

Conventional fold-out maps work just fine when you're planning your trip on the kitchen table, but have you ever tried to use one – or the half-dozen you sometimes need to cover a country – while you're actually on the road? Even if you have the origami skills necessary to unfold the sucker, you know that flimsy bit of paper is not going to last the distance.

"Lonely Planet travel atlases are designed to make it through your journey in one piece – the sturdy book format is based on the assumption that since all travellers want to make it home without punctures, tears or wrinkles, the maps they use should too."

The travel atlases contain detailed, colour maps that are checked on the road by our travel authors to ensure their accuracy. Place name spellings are consistent with our associated guidebooks, so you can use the atlas and the guidebook hand in hand as you travel and find what you are looking for. Unlike conventional maps, each atlas has a comprehensive index, as well as a detailed legend and helpful 'getting around' sections translated into five languages. Sorry, no free steak knives...

Features of this series include:

- full-colour maps, plus colour photos
- maps researched and checked by Lonely Planet authors
- place names correspond with Lonely Planet guidebooks, so there are no confusing spelling differences
- complete index of features and place names
- atlas legend and travelling information presented in five languages: English, French, German, Spanish and Japanese

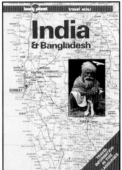

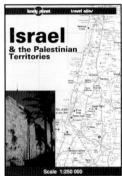

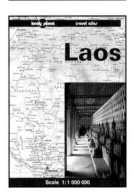

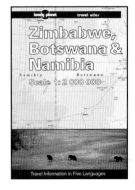

THE LONELY PLANET STORY

Lonely Planet published its first book in 1973 in response to the numerous 'How did you do it?' questions Maureen and Tony Wheeler were asked after driving, bussing, hitching, sailing and railing their way from England to Australia.

Written at a kitchen table and hand collated, trimmed and stapled, *Across Asia on the Cheap* became an instant local bestseller, inspiring thoughts of another book.

Eighteen months in South-East Asia resulted in their second guide, *South-East Asia on a shoestring*, which they put together in a backstreet Chinese hotel in Singapore in 1975. The 'yellow bible', as it quickly became known to backpackers around the world, soon became *the* guide to the region. It has sold well over half a million copies and is now in its 8th edition, still retaining its familiar yellow cover.

Today there are over 180 titles, including travel guides, walking guides, language kits & phrasebooks, travel atlases and travel literature. The company is one of the largest travel publishers in the world. Although Lonely Planet initially specialised in guides to Asia, we now cover most regions of the world, including the Pacific, North America, South America, Africa, the Middle East and Europe.

The emphasis continues to be on travel for independent travellers. Tony and Maureen still travel for several months of each year and play an active part in the writing, updating and quality control of Lonely Planet's guides.

They have been joined by over 70 authors and 170 staff at our offices in Melbourne (Australia), Oakland (USA), London (UK) and Paris (France). Travellers themselves also make a valuable contribution to the guides through the feedback we receive in thousands of letters each year.

The people at Lonely Planet strongly believe that travellers can make a positive contribution to the countries they visit, both through their appreciation of the countries' culture, wildlife and natural features, and through the money they spend. In addition, the company makes a direct contribution to the countries and regions it covers. Since 1986 a percentage of the income from each book has been donated to ventures such as famine relief in Africa; aid projects in India; agricultural projects in Central America; Greenpeace's efforts to halt French nuclear testing in the Pacific; and Amnesty International.

'I hope we send people out with the right attitude about travel. You realise when you travel that there are so many different perspectives about the world, so we hope these books will make people more interested in what they see.'

– Tony Wheeler

LONELY PLANET PUBLICATIONS

AUSTRALIA (HEAD OFFICE)
PO Box 617, Hawthorn 3122, Victoria
tel: (03) 9819 1877   fax: (03) 9819 6459
e-mail: talk2us@lonelyplanet.com.au

UK
10 Barley Mow Passage,
Chiswick, London W4 4PH
tel: (0181) 742 3161 fax: (0181) 742 2772
e-mail: 100413.3551@compuserve.com

USA
Embarcadero West,155 Filbert St, Suite 251,
Oakland, CA 94607
tel: (510) 893 8555   TOLL FREE: 800 275-8555
fax: (510) 893 8563
e-mail: info@lonelyplanet.com

FRANCE
71 bis rue du Cardinal Lemoine, 75005 Paris
tel: 1 44 32 06 20   fax: 1 46 34 72 55
e-mail: 100560.415@compuserve.com

World Wide Web: http://www.lonelyplanet.com/

JORDAN, SYRIA & LEBANON TRAVEL ATLAS

Dear Traveller,

We would appreciate it if you would take the time to write your thoughts on this page and return it to a Lonely Planet office. Only with your help can we continue to make sure this atlas is as accurate and travel-friendly as possible.

Where did you acquire this atlas?

Bookstore ☐   In which section of the store did you find it, i.e. maps or travel guidebooks? ....

Map shop ☐   Direct mail ☐   Other ....

How are you using this travel atlas?

On the road ☐   For home reference ☐   For business reference ☐

Other ....

When travelling with this atlas, did you find any inaccuracies?

....

....

....

How does the atlas fare on the road in terms of ease of use and durability?

....

Are you using the atlas in conjunction with an LP guidebook/s?   Yes ☐   No ☐

Which one/s?..

Have you bought any other LP products for your trip?...

Do you think the information on the travel atlas maps is presented clearly?   Yes ☐   No ☐

If English is not your main language, do you find the language sections useful?   Yes ☐   No ☐

Please list any features you think should be added to the travel atlas.

....

....

....

Would you consider purchasing another atlas in this series?   Yes ☐   No ☐

Please indicate your age group.

15-25 ☐   26-35 ☐   36-45 ☐   46-55 ☐   56-65 ☐   66+ ☐

Do you have any other general comments you'd like to make?

....

....

....

....

....

P.S. Thank you very much for this information. The best contributions will be rewarded with a free copy of a Lonely Planet book. We give away lots of books, but, unfortunately, not every contributor receives one.

Notes

Notes